Science Fair
Survival Techniques

for kids, parents, and teachers

The Balloon Blow·r·upper

the **Wild Goose** company

Real Science—Real Fun!®

Materials & Supplies should be readily available at hardware, hobby, or school supply stores. However, if you are having difficulty finding some of the supplies required for these experiments, you may call the Wild Goose Co. for help in locating the supplies you need.

Plan of Action

Asking the Right Question	4
Reports vs. Experiments	6
How Do I Do an Experiment?	6
The Scientific Method	9
Think of an Idea	9
Research Your Topic	9
Plan Your Experiment	10
Do the Experiment	10
Collect and Record Data	10
Come To a Conclusion	10
A Word About Safety	11

Orienteering

Heavy Metal	15
Drum Roll	17
A Sound Idea	19
Race I (Balloon 500)	21
Race II (Balloon 1000)	23
Race III (Rubber Band 500)	27
Paddle Boat	29
Precision Pocket Plane	32
The Pulse and the Pendulum	34
The Control Panel	38
Invisible Invaders	43
Hero's Engine	46
Liquid Time	48
Drip Time	50
Magic Circles and Square Bubbles	52
Monsoon Measure	55

On Your Own

Classic Guitar	61
The Beat	66
Glob Lobber	68
Sticky Fingers	69
Go With the Flow	70
Rubber Band 1000	71
Foam Boat 1000	73
Bath Time Balance	75
Bath Time Projectiles	77
Sinkable Styrofoam	79
Clay Boats & Ocean Liners	82
Clay Heads and Keels	83
Long Range Water	85
Tense Water	87
Rubber Bands and Steel Girders	89
An Eye for Your Eye	92
Take a Breather	96
Sun Time	99
Heat Wave - Cold Front	102
Take the Pressure	104
Speedy Breezolas	106
Bumpin' Washers	109
Gravity Puzzles & Projectiles	111
Balloon Rockets	113
Running the Rapids	115
Suds & Duds	118
Gas It Up	120
Hey Copper	122
Electric Symphony	124
Talk about Charisma	126
Let There Be Light	128
Color Your Thinking	131
Earthbake	135
Pinstriping the Globe	138
Gooey Glue Globs	139
Slime á la Mode	141
Carbo Goo	143

© 1997 Rev 1999 The Wild Goose Co.

Plan of Action

__ Plan of Action __

You're reading this book for one of three reasons: 1) you're a student looking for ideas for a science fair project; 2) you're a parent who has a student who's bugging you nonstop for ideas; 3) or you're a teacher who has twenty-five students who are bugging you nonstop for ideas for a science fair project. Whatever your situation, science fair time can be as troubling and stressful as it is fun. "Gotta find a project, complete a neat experiment, get wonderful results, and then present the project so it's pretty enough to occupy a space at the Smithsonian." Well, the Wild Goose is here to get rid of all the stress you're going through. Here are guidelines on choosing a project, lots of activities to get you going, and a whole bunch of suggestions for science-like questions to ask about the activities.

If you need help getting started and are a bit clueless as to how to go about a science fair project, then it would be a good idea for you to wade through the following introductory section. You'll learn how to ask the right question, the difference between reports and experiments, the scientific method, and how to do the actual planning and execution of your experiment. If you're an old hand at this stuff and are just looking for new ideas, go ahead and jump to the next two sections (Orienteering and On Your Own) that contain the activities.

By the way, this book is written to the students who are looking for projects. If you're an adult helping a student, you can make the appropriate translations.

Asking the Right Question

Okay, so the teacher walks in and tells the class it's time to start thinking about science fair projects. Let's see, Susy Starfire built that working model of a nuclear reactor last year and Bobby Smarts discovered a new species of wombat and Brittany Bashmore found a cure for the common cold. What *will* you do? What *will* you do? For starters, quit thinking you have to do a project that looks like something from a research lab. Your project doesn't have to be earth-shattering, it doesn't have to involve test tubes and fancy laboratory equipment, and it doesn't have to look like something Al Einstein would have been gaga over. It should be something that *you* are interested in. Having said that, see if the following conversation doesn't sound familiar:

You: "I don't know what to do for my science fair project." (Add whining sounds if appropriate.)

Adult (parent or teacher): "Well, what are you interested in?"

You: "I don't know." (Keep up those whining sounds.)

Adult: "Well, there must be something you're interested in."

You: "I don't know."

Adult: "Well here, look at this list of projects and choose one."

You (thinking): "Yeah boy, those sure do look interesting . . . . **not**."

That kind of conversation takes place every year in just about every school and kitchen in the country. There are some unspoken words, however, that are part of many of those conversations, and they're included in [brackets] and in this version.

You: "I don't know what to do [that looks like some experiment I'd find in a science textbook] for my science fair project." (Add whining sounds if appropriate.)

Adult (parent or teacher): "Well, what are you interested in [that also happens to look like something you'd find in your science textbook]?"

You: "I don't know. [I could never come up with an idea for one of those experiments in the textbook.] (Keep up those whining sounds.)"

Adult: "Well, there must be something you're interested in [that looks like a textbook experiment]."

You: "I don't know."

Adult: "Well here, look at this list of projects and choose one."

You (thinking): "Yeah boy, those sure do look interesting . . . . **not**!"

The problem here is that experiments that you find in textbooks are finished products, and the conclusion to the experiment is well known. Also, they don't show you all the different ways that things can "go wrong," all the problems that emerge, the variables to consider, and all the things that people tried in developing those experiments. Most of all, those experiments reflect someone else's interests. Scientists do experiments because they want to know the answer to a burning question. If you don't really want to know the answer to a question, it's going to be hard to put forth any effort in trying to answer the question.

As an example, consider the following question that will be addressed by two hundred gazillion science fair projects this year. Which of the four major brands of batteries lasts the longest? It's not too difficult to set up an experiment to answer that question, but chances are that most of the kids answering that question don't really care what the answer is. What kind of battery you buy depends on how much money you have to spend, and it's generally true that you get what you pay for. So if you can afford more expensive batteries, they'll probably last longer. Do you really *care* if the Energizer Bunny™ or some other character goes on forever?

Compare that question to this one: Does chewing gum in class help kids do better on tests? This is an actual question addressed in a science fair project! Now the girl who tried to answer this question definitely was interested in the answer. If the answer came out "yes," then she had a great argument to present to her teacher. That is, if chewing gum helps you relax enough to do better on tests, then everyone should be allowed to chew gum in class. Now there's a result worth going after!

Not every question can be addressed with a scientific investigation, but you might be surprised at those that can. Here are a few examples of questions that are the starting point for an experiment:

- Do different-colored M&Ms taste different?
- How much TV do the kids in my class watch, and why?
- Does doing homework really help you learn better?
- What kind of cat litter needs to be changed the least often?
- Does eating snacks with lots of sugar really make you hyperactive?

Notice that none of these questions are your typical "science geek" questions. You're more likely to enjoy your science fair project if you stay away from the questions you think the adults want you to ask.

Reports versus Experiments

Here are a few more questions others have considered for science fair projects:

- How does a water treatment plant work?
- What is the life cycle of a frog?
- Is smoking bad for you?
- What is the strongest material known to humans?
- What is the universe made of?

If you've been around science fairs before, you'll recognize these as projects kids have done (you perhaps?). The problem with these questions, though, is that to find the answers, all you have to do is look them up. Scientists have already answered these questions, and you can find those answers in encyclopedias, textbooks, and magazines. So, what you end up with is a **report** instead of an **experiment**. Many schools won't allow reports as entries into science fairs, but then many schools do allow them. In fact, a glitzy report can sometimes win a science fair. In order to understand what scientists do, however, you ought to do experiments rather than reports. Besides, they're much more fun! Of course, maybe you're not really sure what an experiment is. If that's the case, read on.

How do I do an Experiment?

Here is an example of the correct way to do an experiment using the chewing gum. As you go along, you'll notice that things start out simple but quickly get complicated. That always happens when you have an interesting question to answer, so don't worry about it. If you can set up an experiment without any trouble and without anything going wrong, you probably have a simple, not-so-interesting question to answer.

Okay, you want to know what effect chewing gum has on your test performance. Suppose you start with the following simple experiment:

First you take a math test while chewing gum. Then you take the same math test while not chewing gum. You then find out which time you got a better score on the test.

Before deciding whether or not this is a good experiment, here's a new term for you. A *variable* is anything that can possibly change the outcome of an experiment. One obvious variable is whether or not you chew gum while taking the test. Below are some others to consider:

the time of day

> how tired you are

> how hard the test is

the subject matter (math, spelling, etc.) of the test

> the temperature in the room when you take the test

> the day of the week you take the test

the amount of exercise you had just before taking the test

> . . . . and there's more!

The key to a good experiment is keeping *all* of the variables the same except the one you're testing (chewing gum or not). For example, if you take the gum-chewing test in the morning and the non-gum-chewing test in the afternoon, it's possible that you would do poorly on the non-gum-chewing test because you were tired, not because you weren't chewing gum. Or maybe you decide to take a math test while chewing gum and a reading test while not chewing gum. If you do better on one of the tests, is it because of gum chewing or because you're better at math than reading? By the way, there's a name for keeping all variables except the one you're interested in constant. It's called **controlling variables**.

Let's rethink the chewing gum experiment, trying to control all the variables. You have to take one test while chewing gum and a second test while not chewing gum. First, take a math test each time. Then you should make sure you take the two tests at the same time of day, so you'll have to take the tests on different days, say at 2:00 P.M. Since you're taking tests on different days, why not take them on successive Mondays (maybe you do better on tests on different days of the week). Also, make sure you have the same number of hours of sleep the night before each test. Make sure the temperature in the room is the same each time, and do the same amount of exercise the morning before each test.

Getting the idea it's not always easy to control variables? Welcome to real science! One thing nice about controlling variables, though, is that you don't have to worry about *all* the variables in the world. For example, the color of shirt you're wearing probably won't affect test results. Neither will the kind of pencil you use or the way you do your hair in the morning. You only need to worry about variables that might directly affect the results of the test.

So far so good, but you can still improve the experiment quite a bit. One variable you haven't controlled yet has to do with the fact that you take the same test each time. That variable is whether or not you've already taken the test. The first time, you haven't seen the test before, and the second time you have. The way to fix that is to give yourself different tests each time. Of course, those tests have to be of the same difficulty. How will you manage that? It's actually not so easy to do, but then you already know that interesting science questions cause you to run into a few snags here and there.

A great way to make your experiment and results better is to do **repeat trials**. That means do the experiment lots of times to see if you get consistent results. If you do the experiment only once, then you can't be sure that it will turn out the same way each time. If you get the same results fifty times in a row, though, you might be on to something.

Another way to improve this experiment is to get yourself out of the picture. It's usually not a good idea for the experimenter to be tested in his or her own experiment. You might tend to perform differently on the tests because you want the experiment to come out a certain way (now what result might that be?). So, when humans are involved in your experiment, you should use people other than yourself. You could choose one friend and have him do the experiment twenty times, or you could choose twenty friends and have them do the experiment once each. Which one sounds easier? Choosing twenty friends, of course. You might even try giving half the kids a test while they chew gum and the other half the same test while not chewing gum. That controls one variable for you (not having to worry about getting two tests that are equally hard), but it creates another one. Suppose the half that chews gum is, on the average, a lot better at math than the half that doesn't chew gum? If you do the half and half thing, you have to find a way to make sure your two groups have equal math abilities. Once again, that solution is up to you to figure out.

A few things should now be clear from the discussion of the chewing gum experiment. One is that an experiment that might seem simple at first usually turns out to be not so simple. It's sometimes almost impossible to control all the variables (how do you make sure that twenty people get the same amount of sleep the night before the test?). It can also be very difficult figuring out how to control even *some* of the variables. Then, when you get your results, they don't always make sense. It could easily take a professional scientist six months to a year (!) to come up with a good experimental design and results for the gum-chewing experiment. There are lots of stops along the way to solve problems that you didn't think of when you started the experiment. In a science fair project, though, you don't have a long time. You have a couple of choices as to what to do about that. One is that you could get through the experiment, not control all the variables (maybe because you couldn't figure out how), and come up with *some* kind of result (that may or may not make sense). The second is to go about the experiment as a scientist would, solving problems along the way. This second option means you probably won't finish your experiment. Which option you choose depends on what you, your parents, and your teachers want to end up with after a month or two spent on a project. The second option is recommended because it's more like what real scientists do. But if your school wants something else, that that's the way to go.

The Scientific Method

Most people who run science fairs ask you to report on your project using the Scientific Method. The Scientific Method guides you through your project by providing a number of steps to follow. Here's a simple version:

1. Think of an idea.
2. Research your topic.
3. Plan your experiment.
4. Do the experiment.
5. Collect and record data.
6. Come to a conclusion.

Now if you have to report your project in this format, that's fine. Real science is seldom done in this step by step fashion, but let's discuss these steps one at a time so you have a starting point.

Think of an Idea

Well, this obviously comes first, but not without a bit of mental messing around. Maybe you already have a burning question you want answered, but often you have to just try messing around with things before a question pops into your head. Suppose you like working with plants. To think of an experiment having to do with plants, you could just start looking at plants closely, taking them apart, watching how they grow, and things like that. Along the way, you might start asking yourself things like "I wonder why this plant has a yellow leaf and that one has a green leaf," or "How much trimming is good for a plant, and at what point does more trimming cause the plant harm?" Okay, okay, those may not be the questions *you'd* think of. Come up with your own. The point is that good experimental questions don't just find their way to your brain while you're watching TV. "Think of an idea" involves a lot of doing.

Research Your Topic

This is a tough one. Sometimes it's just about impossible to research your topic. Seen any books about gum chewing and test taking lately? Most often, though, there's a whole lot written about whatever your project topic is. In fact, you could spend *months* just reading up on your topic. If you read a lot about your topic, you'll become more informed and you'll learn a lot, but something else might happen. Because books tend to present everything known about a topic, rather than what is not known, you can get the impression that there's no way you could come up with an interesting question that doesn't already have an answer. It's a good idea to write down what you know and what you want to find out before you do a lot of research. It also wouldn't hurt to start some experimenting before doing a lot of reading. That way, when you do your research, you can narrow your work down to things that relate to your experiment.

Plan Your Experiment

Definitely a good idea if you're going to do an experiment! Planning means figuring out what **variables** you want to control and exactly how you're going to do the experiment. After you've planned the experiment, do a quick trial of the experiment, without making a big deal of controlling all the variables or taking really careful data. In this "test run," you'll most likely discover variables you hadn't thought of and a whole bunch of problems in collecting information. Use what you find in your test run to redesign the experiment. After a few trials, you'll probably be ready to do a full-scale experiment and collect real data.

Do the Experiment

No, duh! This step is here just in case you forget that you're supposed to be doing an experiment. Plan on doing the experiment several times. Things seldom work the first time through. Besides, you'll want to test general variables several times to make sure you know what to expect.

Collect and Record Data

This is really just part of doing the experiment. The important thing in collecting information is to write it down and be sure to label everything well. Maybe you think you'll remember what those numbers on the back of your notebook mean, but those things can slip your mind two weeks later. It's a real pain to have to re-do your experiment because you forgot who got what score, which bunny rabbit ate the most, how many seconds it took the green slime to stretch a foot, or whatever.

Come to a Conclusion

Sounds like a nice way to end an experiment, but it can be very difficult to conclude anything based on *one* experiment. Most the time, one experiment lets you know that you need to do about five more experiments before you can come to a complete conclusion. That's okay though. Just state what you learned from the experiment you did, how it could be improved, and what questions you now have as a result of doing the one experiment. Accept the fact that no, you probably don't have a complete answer to your question yet.

Science should be safe as well as fun, so whenever you're in the lab or practicing a little home experimentation, there are some important precautions you should always keep in mind. Never eat or drink in your laboratory. Read all the directions before you begin any experiment and if you aren't sure about something, ask an adult! Watch out for small pieces, balloons or rubber bands that may be part of your materials. Not only are they easy to lose but they can be a choking danger to young children or pets who might try to swallow them. Never be careless in the lab, rough play can lead to spills, fires, broken equipment and injuries. Always be careful with chemicals and always, always be a clean scientist. So have fun, be safe, and how 'bout giving us a little credit when you collect your Nobel Prize.

GENERAL CHEMICAL SAFETY

EYES: Rinse immediately with water. Remove contact lenses if any; flush eyes with water for 15 minutes.

SWALLOWED: Rinse mouth. Drink a glassful of water or milk. DO NOT INDUCE VOMITING.

SKIN: Flush skin thoroughly with water.

In all cases, if an emergency exists, get immediate medical attention.

Orienteering

The rest of this book is filled with lots of activities cooked up at the Goose. The activities themselves would not necessarily make good science fair projects. There's a section at the end of each activity that lists possible science fair questions to ask that are related to the activity, along with a list of the variables you might need to control in doing an experiment. In other words, these activities are intended to get you started, not to provide a ready-made experiment for you. Each activity has a materials list, a step-by-step procedure, and an explanation of what's going on (the science stuff).

You might do an activity that looks interesting (none of them take a great deal of time) in order to "get your feet wet" (that's what wild geese do), learn a bit about the subject matter of the activity, and see if you'd like to do an experiment based on the activity. If none of the questions provided grab your interest, make up your own (those are the best anyway) or move on to another activity. If you do all the activities in the book and still don't find one that gets your blood flowing, there's always that unanswered question about chewing gum and tests . . .

Activity 1   Heavy Metal

Materials

   1 big Slinky™ or Slinky Jr.™ (a long floppy spring works too)
   1 metal rod (12" long and ¼" in diameter - get at hardware store - or
       the longest ½" bolt you can find - must be at least 8" long)
   1 table knife

Procedure

1. Hold the center of the metal rod tightly between your thumb and forefinger.

2. Strike the end of the rod with your table knife. You can also tap the end of the rod on a hard surface. Do you hear a nice bell tone? If not, move your fingers down just a tiny bit and try again. You'll know when your fingers are positioned correctly because if they're not, you'll hear a big thud instead of a nice ping.

3. Now hold the rod about ¼ of the way down its length and rap it again with your table knife. Move your fingers around until you get a ring instead of a thud. The ring you get this time should have a higher pitch than the one you got before.

hold this
end →

move this
↲ end

fundametal
wave

4. Experiment with pitch by holding the rod in different places and tapping it.   You'll hear various notes.

5. What's going on in this metal mystery?

Explanation

This explanation requires you to do some things with the Slinky™ (in the text it's called a spring), so grab it before you go any further. Lay it on a hard floor or smooth table. Take one end of the spring in each hand and, by moving one end up and down, create the pattern above . This is called a **fundamental** wave pattern. The number of times you move the end of the spring up and down in a second is called the **frequency** of vibration. If you move your hand up and down faster, that's an increase in frequency.

   Move the spring even faster (increase the frequency) until you get a pattern like the second one shown. Notice that it has two sections that move up and down. This pattern of vibration is called the **first harmonic.** Increase the frequency even more until you get a pattern with three sections moving up and down. No surprise that this pattern is called the **second harmonic.**

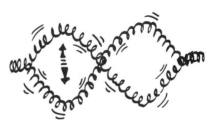

first frequency

Science Fair Survival Techniques

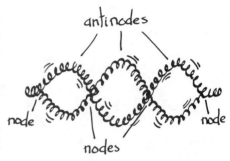

What you've just created are called standing waves and no, they don't have tiny feet. The name comes from the fact that parts of the wave don't move at all while other parts move like crazy. The parts that don't move at all are called **nodes** and that parts that move a lot are called **antinodes.**

Anytime you pluck or whack something, it vibrates into a whole bunch of standing wave patterns. When you pluck a rubber band (try it!) or a string on a guitar, it might look like it's only vibrating in a fundamental pattern. But the other patterns (first and second harmonics, plus others) are also created; you just don't see them very well. Vibrations cause sound, which is why a plucked string makes noise. The faster the vibration, the higher the frequency, and the higher the note. So something vibrating slowly produces low notes (called a low **pitch**) and something vibrating quickly produces high notes (a high pitch)

OK, now let's bring the metal rod into all this harmony. When you hit the metal rod, it vibrates and produces sound. Keep in mind that you can't really see the vibrations because they're much too small for your eyes but not for your ears. When you hold the rod with your fingers, you keep part of the rod from vibrating. By holding the rod, you're forcing that point on the rod to be a node. When this happens, it limits the kind of standing waves that can form when you whack the rod. This in turn determines the frequency and pitch of the sound you hear.

If you hold the rod off-center, you keep a different part of the rod from vibrating. At this point, the standing wave you were able to produce before can't really get going because your hand acts as a block. However, other standing waves are able to get started. This standing wave has a higher frequency than the first one, so you have a higher pitch. When you hold the rod in different places, you allow some of the standing waves to occur and you prevent others from happening. This results in different notes. Just like Poseidon, that Greek god of the sea, you control the waves . . . not sea waves, sound waves.

Science Fair Suggestions

To turn this into a science fair project, all you have to do is come up with some questions that don't have obvious answers. Some questions and the variables you'd have to control are listed below.

1. What material is best for producing really nice sounds when you whack it? For this question, you should replace the metal rod with rods made of plastic, wood, and metals other than the one you just used. Variables to control: length of rod, diameter of rod, shape of rod, object you hit the rod with, how hard you hit the rod, person who judges the tone quality, and where you hold the rod each time.

2. What diameter rod produces the most pleasing sounds? Obviously, you'll need to try rods of many different diameters. Variables to control: length of rod, material rod is made of, how hard you hit the rod, shape of rod, object you hit the rod with, person who judges the tone quality, and where you hold the rod each time.

Activity 2   Drum Roll

Materials
　　3　balloons
　　2　paper tubes
　　1　pencil
　　　　clear tape
　　　　flour or powder
　　　　salt
　　　　scissors

Procedure

1. Cut the neck off of two balloons and toss the balloon necks into the trash. Tightly stretch one of the leftover balloon tops over each end of the paper tube. You might want to use tape to hold the balloons in place.

2. Use the pencil to tap one end of the drum you just created. Okay, it doesn't exactly sound like an expensive drum, but at least the sound is consistent.

3. Grab your salt and sprinkle an even amount over the balloon surface of the drum. Start tapping the drum again with your pencil. Keep tapping until you notice that the salt starts to collect in certain places on the drum head and forms a pattern.

4. Tap the drum surface in a different spot and see if the salt pattern changes.

5. Get rid of the salt and sprinkle flour or powder evenly across the surface. Start tapping again. What difference is there between the pattern of the salt and the pattern of the flour?

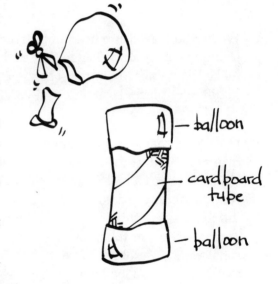

Music Theory

Real drum heads (and even balloons stretched over paper tubes) vibrate when you hit them. As you probably expected, the drum head vibration creates the sounds you hear. With what you've discovered already, did you realize that the drum head vibrates in a *standing wave*? The only difference is that this standing wave is <u>two</u>-dimensional and it can get a little complicated because some parts of the drum head move up and down frequently (antinodes) while some parts don't move at all (nodes).

When you strike the drum head with salt on the surface, the salt that's on the antinodes gets bounced around and eventually winds up on the stationary nodes. What you end up with is a pattern called a **Chaladni Figure,** which shows you just what the drum head's standing wave looks like. The powder or flour creates a different pattern because it tends to collect at the antinodes instead of at the nodes. It is so light, in fact, that the air just above the drum head moves it towards the antinodes.

Science Fair Survival Techniques

Science Fair Suggestions

1. How do the Chaladni patterns on a real drum change as you change the tension on the drum head? In order to address this question, you obviously have to have access to a real drum on which you can change the tension. If you have that access, then you'll have to figure out a way to change the tension of the drum head in a consistent way. That's not such an easy thing to do, but it makes for a fun challenge. Once you figure that out, you'll have to control the following variables: which drum you use (use the same one each time), how hard you hit the drum head to create the pattern, how many times you hit the drum head, where on the drum head you hit it, what you use to hit the drum (a drum stick? duh), who hits the drum, what and how much powder or salt you use to create the pattern, and the humidity (the drier the air, the less the powder and salt clump). A neat follow-up to this question is whether or not there's a pattern to the change in Chaladni patterns. In other words, can you look at a pattern and tell what the tension of the drum is?

2. When you hit a drum head in different places, it makes different sounds. Do the Chaladni patterns change as the sound changes? If so, how? Can you predict what pattern a given sound is going to make? Variables to control: The same as for the first question, except that you'll want to hit the drum in different places each time and you'll want to keep the tension the same each time.

3. How does changing the diameter of the drum head affect the Chaladni pattern? You don't need a real drum for this one. Just different sized balloons and different sized things to stretch them over (toilet paper tubes, metal or plastic cans, etc.). Variables to control: The thickness of the balloon (you'll need larger balloons to make larger drum heads, but sometimes larger balloons are thicker), how tight the drum head is (not easy to control), whether your support for the drum head is open at both ends or closed at one end, where and how hard you hit the drum head, and what material (salt? powder?) you use to make the pattern.

Activity 3   A Sound Idea

Materials

2 paper cups	1 nail
2 paper clips	1 piece tissue paper
1 friend	1 rubber band
1 length of string	

Procedure

1. With a partner, work on a counter top or table to do this part. Place your ear on the table so that it's pressed down firmly. Put a finger in your other ear. Have the other person stand at the far end of the surface and *lightly* tap it with a finger. Count the taps. Now, have them use the nail and try to tap so quietly that you can't hear it. Stand up straight and have them repeat the taps with both finger and nail. Listen carefully but keep moving farther away until you can't hear the taps. Try this on a long, hard surface such as a wooden handrail or metal fence until you're about fifty feet apart or more.

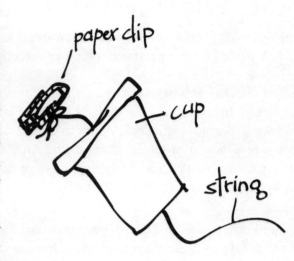

2. Have your friend stand in one room and you in another so that an inside wall is between you. The other person is reading out loud. Stand away from the wall and try to hear the words. Move closer until your ear is pressed against the wall and listen for the words.

3. Use the nail to poke a small hole in the bottom of each cup. Thread the string though each hole and tie it to a paper clip, as shown in the sketch. Each of you take a cup and walk apart until the string is pulled tightly between you. Of course, if you pull too hard you may rip the cups apart. Ah, the perils of technology.

   Have your friend speak into one cup as you listen in the other. Remarkable clarity? Barely audible? Try it with the string hanging loosely. With the string tight again, listen as you rub your fingers back and forth along the string. Try plucking the string. Try a different kind of material between the cups if you can. If possible, try getting farther and farther apart and still be able to hear each other. Is there a limit? What if you use fishing line instead of string?

4. Use the rubber band and hold the piece of tissue paper in place over one of the cups. Pull the string tight and speak into the tissue paper cup as your friend listens on the other end. Trade places and repeat. Notice any difference in sound quality.

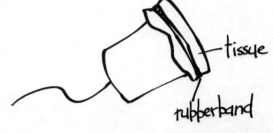

Science Fair Survival Techniques

Explanation

Vibrations cause sound by compressing and releasing molecules in wavelike patterns. Unlike light, these vibrations (called sound waves) require a form of matter through which to pass. The most common medium for sound vibrations is air, but as you have just demonstrated, sound waves can travel much better through a solid medium such as string, wood or steel. This is because on average the molecules of matter are closer together in solids than in gasses. Vibrations do very nicely in water, too, as shown by animals that communicate many miles with low-frequency grunts, whistles and echoes. The quality of the sound waves depends greatly on the quality of the medium. Changing the medium will change the sound quality. No doubt you noticed this when changing the tightness of the string, using a different kind of line, covering the cup with tissue paper or tapping steel and then wood.

Science Fair Suggestions

String and cup telephones have been around for a long time, so don't expect a lot of praise if you just put one together for your project. Better to investigate one of the questions below.

1. What material is best to use as a string for this telephone? You could try different sizes and weights of string, fishing line, and various kinds of wire. You'll also have to figure out what *best* means. Loudest? Best tone quality? Ability to understand words? Variables to control: What you use for the cups, how you connect the *string* to the cups, who evaluates the quality of transmission, who does the speaking (if you use a person), amount of extraneous noise around, length of *string*, and how tight the *string* is (difficult to control).

2. What kind, shape, and size of *cup* makes for the best telephone? This is a lot like number 1, but you keep the string type and size constant while changing the material, size, and shape of the cup (you'd have to do a different experiment for each of these).

3. Is there a limit to how long the string can be? Is that limit different for different materials? To investigate this, just change the length of the string while keeping everything else constant (see number 1 above). You'll need to repeat the experiment with each new material you try for the string.

The next three activities have to do with building race cars. The first activity requires a balloon racer. It will give you a little background on the motion of race cars. The two activities that follow Race 1 are the ones to concentrate on if you're looking for a full-blown science fair project.

Activity 4   Race I (Balloon 500)

Materials

1 set of lungs
1 sheet of paper
1 stick of clay

1 toy balloon racer
clear tape

Procedure

1. Inspect your racer and make sure there are no sharp edges that can pop your balloon when you begin blowing it up.

2. Make sure your balloon is correctly positioned inside the car.

3. Inflate the balloon on the car by blowing through the nozzle at the back. Be sure and plug the nozzle with your finger or you'll lose all your power (air). Duh!

4. Set the car on a smooth, level surface and let go. Unless you placed the car upside down, it should go somewhere. Practice this several times to get more distance.

Explanation

Any object, like a toy car, needs a push to get it moving. The technical name for that push is force. The question to ponder is, "Where exactly did that push come from to move the balloon racer?" The balloon didn't do anything except deflate. Why should that push the racer? It all has to do with **Newton's Third Law.** The law goes like this: when an object is pushed or pulled, it pushes or pulls back with an equal but opposite force. You push on a wall, it pushes back. A rock falls on your head, your head hits the rock with an equal force. (However, for some reason, it hurts you more than it hurts the rock. The rock seems pretty nonchalant about the whole thing.) When you let go of the balloon, it deflates to get back to its original state. As it does this, it pushes air out the back end of the racer and that's the key. When air is being pushed out of the racer, the air pushes back on the racer, causing it to go forward. This is exactly how a jet engine works. It pushes hot gases towards the rear of the jet, and those gases push back, causing the jet to accelerate forward. Rockets do the same thing. Before you qualify for the next race, let's try some extra laps with your balloon racer.

Science Fair Survival Techniques

Extensions

1. Try your balloon racer on various surfaces and see if it performs differently.

2. Add various amounts of modeling clay to the body of your balloon racer and see how the motion is affected. If you try this adjustment, the next race will make miles more sense.

3. Make a paper nose cone for your racer and attach it to the front of your car with clear tape. This might reduce air resistance and make it go farther. What other improvements can you think of?

Science Fair Suggestions

There is a certain size balloon that will get the car to go as far as possible. What size is that? A very small balloon won't give you much push, and a very large balloon makes the whole contraption too heavy to move. Somewhere in between must be the perfect balloon size. Variables to control: the surface the car is on, how level the surface is, the wind speed (if you're doing it outside), and whether or not the wheels slip.

Activity 5 Race II (Balloon 1000)

Materials:

8 flat nuts (hardware store)
4 plastic bottle caps (plastic milk jug caps will do)
4 slip nuts
2 balloons
2 straws
2 wooden dowels
1 adult pit crew chief
1 candle
1 crescent wrench or pair of pliers

1 large nail
1 pair of scissors or serrated table knife
1 pen or pencil
1 plastic bottle, 20 oz.
1 push pin
1 stick of clay
  matches
  clear tape

Procedure

1. The alignment of the axles is *very* important. It could even become one of the variables you test. The holes you make need to be carefully placed so that the axles are parallel to and on the same level as each other. The first hole can be just about anywhere; it's the remaining three that have to be measured and placed carefully!

2. Using the push pin, poke pilot holes in the bottle at the points where you've chosen to place your four axle holes. While you're at it, use your push pin to poke a hole in the center of each of the four plastic bottle caps.

3. Use the large nail to poke holes in the same place where you made the small push pin holes. Shove the nail through each of the four marks in the bottle and remove the nail. This is demonstrated in the drawing on the next page.

4. Use the large nail again to poke holes in the middle of each of the plastic bottle caps. It's important that you push the nail through *from the inside* of the cap *towards the outside*. You may have to twist the nail a little in order to do this. **Hold the cap in a way that prevents you from poking yourself with the nail.** Remove the nail after you've made a hole in all four caps. You may need help from an adult. Check the drawing.

5. You may need to ask for some assistance from an adult in this next step. Have your assistant hold a lit candle to provide a flame. Hold the sharp end of the nail in the top part of the flame for about a minute. You should be holding the nail by the *head* so you don't get burned. However, if for some reason your end of the nail heats up, by all means **DROP THE NAIL!** That's a no-brainer.

plastic cap
nail

6. After a minute, remove the nail from the flame and immediately push it through one of the nail holes you made in the bottle. The plastic around the hole should melt away a little bit, enlarging the hole. You can run the nail back and forth through the hole to help the process along. Running the nail through the hole will remove any unsightly plastic goobers that are hanging on and around the plastic edges.

7. Run the heated nail through all four holes in the plastic and extinguish the flame when you're done. **DO NOT POKE THE HEATED NAIL THROUGH THE HOLES IN THE PLASTIC BOTTLE CAPS!!!**

8. Grab your wooden dowels. These are the axles that hold the wheels for your car. Put the dowels (axles) into the holes in the bottle and check that they spin freely. If they're sluggish or get stuck during a spin, you'll have to enlarge the holes in the plastic by using your heated nail. Just make sure you don't enlarge the holes too much.

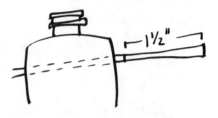

9. Ask your adult assistant to help you again on this step. Use a serrated table knife or scissors and cut off the very bottom of the plastic bottle. Don't cut off too much. Look at your "car" so far. The front of your racer is where the neck of the bottle is located. The rear of the car is the now open end of the bottle.

10. Position the axles (dowels) evenly in the holes. Look to make sure the axles are centered in the bottle (an equal amount sticks out of both sides). Take your ruler and measure 1½ inches from the end of one axle towards the plastic bottle. Make a small mark with your pen at that exact spot on the axle. Repeat this process for the other three axles protruding from the bottle. Take a look at the next drawing.

11. Grab the four round silver slip nuts. The slip nuts are about ¾ inch across and each one has seven tiny slits. With the axles centered in the bottle, push one slip nut onto each of the axles. The flat side of the slip nut should point towards the bottle. Continue pushing the slip nuts up to the marks you made. When you get them all in position, they should each be about ¼ inch from the bottle. Check the diagram.

CAUTION: THE SLIP NUTS GO ONE WAY ONLY!
IF YOU PUSH THEM TOO FAR, YOU'LL NEED A NEW DOWEL.

12. Take a flat nut and make sure the sharp protruding side is facing the bottle. Twist a flat nut onto each axle until the nut is at least 1 inch from the end of the axle. You can try turning the nuts by hand but it requires a lot of strength and it's easy to cut yourself, so be careful. A better idea is to use some pliers or a crescent wrench to rotate the nuts into position.

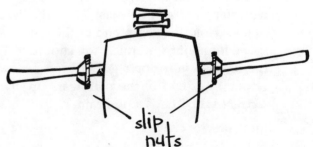

13. Pull out the four plastic bottle caps which will act as your wheels. With the flat side facing the plastic bottle, push them along the axles until they fit snugly against the flat nuts.

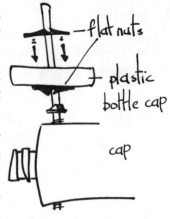

14. Now you need four more flat nuts. Twist a flat nut onto the end of each axle and tighten them against the plastic wheels. The flat side of each nut should sit against the inside of the bottle caps. Take a peek at the drawing.

15. Check to see if your car rolls smoothly across the floor. Make any minor adjustments that are needed. You might need to straighten the wheels so they are aligned.

16. Wahoooo! . . . it's time to add your power. Start by placing a balloon over the end of one of the straws. Now, secure it tightly in place with a thin rubber band.

17. Tape the straw lengthwise to the top of your racer so that the balloon is hanging at the front. (Remember that the narrow neck of the bottle is the front end of your car.) The other end of the straw should extend past the rear of your race car.

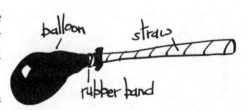

20. Just as you did with the balloon racer, blow up the balloon and hold the end of the straw closed with a finger. Place your car on a smooth surface and let her fly.

21. Okay, so that wasn't exactly Dragsters of Thunder. Let's try attaching a second balloon and straw combo to your car. It might take a bit of practice but you should be able to blow up both balloons, seal them with your fingers, and let them go at the same time. Did that help your car go any faster?

Explanation

Just by holding the previous two cars in your hands (balloon racer and model racer), you can tell your model car is much heavier. You could say that the model car has a larger mass than the balloon racer. Now, don't confuse mass with weight because they're not the same thing. **Mass** is how much "stuff" there is in something. It's important to remember that it is harder to change the motion of something with a large mass. That's why that single balloon was more effective in moving the small-mass race car than the large-mass model car. Of course, adding a second balloon to the model car changes things a little bit. The added balloon means pushing twice as much air out the back. The air pushes back with equal force (Can I interest you in a review of Newton's Third Law?), so you get twice the force pushing the mass of the model car forward.

All this motor madness is summed up in **Newton's Second Law.** This law has a big fat equation attached to it, but don't worry about jotting it down. Let's break down the equation into words. The second law says that for a certain force, a larger mass results in a smaller change in motion. In other words, the model car, which has a large mass, won't go very far when the only force acting on it is the push from a single balloon. From that you can assume that a larger force acting on the same mass will result in a greater change in motion. You've got it! That means that two balloons can move your model car further. So, if you want a car to go fast, you should give it as small a mass as possible and push it with as large a force as possible. Whoever figured out that law has got to be a genius, don't you think? What can you do to build a better car?

Extensions

See if you can use Newton's Second Law of motion to explain why adding modeling clay to the balloon racer slows it down. (Did you change force or mass by adding the clay?) Experiment with changing the mass of the model car and confirm your explanation.

Science Fair Suggestions

This car operates on the same principles as the toy car in the previous activity, but because you put it together yourself, there are lots more questions you can investigate.

1. Is there an ideal number of straws and balloons that make the car go as fast and as far as possible? When you add more balloons, that increases the push you give the car but it also increases the mass you have to move. At what point does the increase in mass overcome the increase in push and actually slow the car down? Variables to control: surface the car is on, amount of wind, amount each balloon is blown up (tough to control!), direction straws are facing (if you nudge one to the side accidentally, it won't push as effectively), and amount of wheel slippage.

2. How can the design of the car be changed to increase the distance it travels? This question requires lots of little experiments. There are many things you can change on this car, such as wheel size, size of the holes for the axles, balloon size, aerodynamics (such as adding a nose cone), materials used for the axles and wheels, type of bottle used, and diameter of straw. To come up with the ultimate design, you could change a whole bunch of things at once, but then you wouldn't know which changes were effective and which weren't. So, you would have to change one thing at a time. Say you want to see how wheel size affects performance. Then you'd have to change just the wheel size and nothing else to see which size wheel is the best. In that case, you'd have to control the following variables: material wheels are made of, type of bottle used, amount balloon is inflated, surface the car is on, and anything else you can think of! In developing the best car, you'll have to be careful about making changes that can't be reversed. For example, if you increase the size of the holes for the axles, you can't make the holes smaller again. What you'd have to do is make about four cars that are identical except for the size of the axle holes.

Activity 6   Race III (Rubber Band 500)

Materials:

Your model car from Race II   1 push pin
1 adult   1 retainer pin
1 candle   1 small nail
1 pair of pliers   matches
1 pen or pencil   thin rubber bands

Procedure

1. Remove the balloons and straws from your model car.

2. You'll be using two, thin rubber bands as the new power source for your car. Loop the rubber bands together in order to make one rubber band about 5½ inches in length. If one rubber band breaks, grab another!

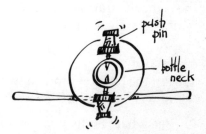

3. Use a pen to mark two holes on either side of the bottle neck. The marks should be directly across from each other and perpendicular to the axles (axles run left and right; this hole goes up and down). Use the push pin to punch two holes through the marks. Don't panic, the drawing will guide you.

4. Take the small nail and grab an adult. Have the adult hold a candle like last time. Take the small nail with pliers and heat the sharp end. Hold your car and gently work the nail through the bottle neck, top to bottom, by using both push pin holes as your guide. Holding your car will prevent you from putting too much pressure on the axles. The head of the nail should be on the top and the sharp end of the nail should stick out the bottom hole. In other words, when you've finished, the sharp end of the nail should be pointing down.

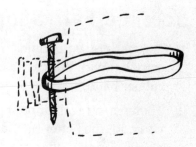

5. Place your rubber band into the neck of the bottle. Pull the nail out of the bottom hole in the neck and hold your rubber band in such a way that it gets hooked on the nail. Push the nail back into place.

6. Snap the retainer pin onto the middle of the rear axle. The rear axle is the one at the open end of your car.

7. Loop the unattached end of the rubber band over the retainer pin so that it catches on the pin. You may have to hold it over the pin to get it to catch on.

8. Now turn the wheels backwards so that the rubber band winds around the rear axle. Keep turning your wheels backwards until the rubber band is tight and you can barely turn the wheels anymore. Don't let go of the wheels or your car engine will unwind!

9. Give your car a test drive. You might notice that there's a lot of slipping and sliding going on.

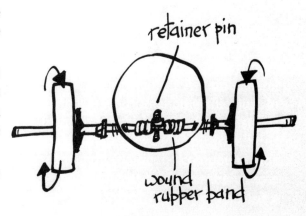

Science Fair Survival Techniques

Explanation

All cars, no matter what size, operate on the principle of **energy transfer**. You added energy to the first car by blowing up the balloon. Keep in mind the energy was stored in the expanded balloon. When the balloon was released and returned to its original shape, at least some of the energy was transferred to the **motion energy** of the car. Even though your car is now rubber band powered, energy transfer is still at work. You added energy to the rubber band by winding up the rear wheels and changing the shape of the rubber band from relaxed to stretched. When you let your car go, the energy in the rubber band went directly into the motion energy of the rear axle and the wheels (They spin!). If the motion of the wheels translated directly to the forward motion of the car, you'd have a perfect system. Unfortunately a lot of the energy is wasted in the transfer.

Extensions

1. Put the balloons and straws back on your car and see if the combination of jet power and rubber band power gives you a faster ride. Unless you have four hands, you may need an assistant on this one.

2. See what results you get on different surfaces and inclines.

Science Fair Suggestions

1. For starters, you could investigate the same question as in the second suggestion for the previous activity. With this car, of course, there are new things to change, such as the size and strength of the rubber band.

2. There is an ideal amount of weight to add to this car to improve its performance. The more weight you add, the better the traction. But adding weight also makes it harder to change the car's motion. At what point does the added weight start to hurt the car's performance? Variables to control: number of turns of the rear axle, size and strength of the rubber band (note that rubber bands tend to lose elasticity over time), surface the car is on, and all the other stuff you had to control for the other cars.

In the two activities that follow, you'll investigate motion in the water and motion in the air.

Activity 7   Paddle Boat

Materials

7 slotted craft sticks   1 large rubber band
5 small rubber bands

Procedure

1. The craft sticks are scored so you can easily break them into shorter pieces. You might want to read twice because you can only break once. Take three of the sticks and break them at the scores nearest the middle, as shown. Set the end pieces aside for now. You'll use them in a minute.

2. Grab two long craft sticks. Use the middle pieces from Step 1 to hold the long sticks in place by anchoring them in the slots as shown. The three cross pieces should be on the top edge of the long sticks. You should have a wooden rectangle divided one-third/two-thirds by the cross pieces.

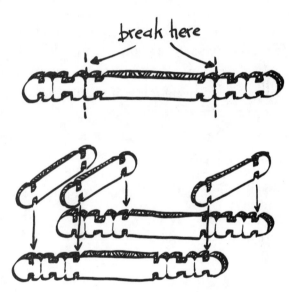

3. Place one large rubber band around the two long sticks in the center of the larger section as shown. It should be loose so don't wrap it at all. This rubber band is your boat's "motor." The wooden rectangle is now evenly divided into thirds.

4. Snag two more long craft sticks and snap them in place on top of the cross pieces to hold the boat together. Make sure the slots interlock snugly so that the long craft sticks touch each other. Flip the wooden box . . . uh, boat, over so that the lone rubber band is on the top level. Your boat is now right-side up!

5. Wrap a small rubber band around the outside of the sticks at each cross piece to keep the whole thing together. Two wraps of each rubber band is good enough. Try to put a wrap on each side of the end of a cross piece. The inside cross piece is a little tricky so you may need some help.

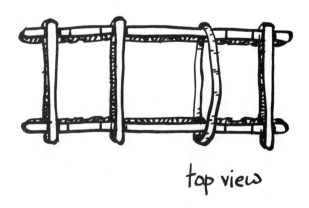

top view

Science Fair Survival Techniques

6. Time to make the paddle wheel for your boat. Get all six end pieces you set aside from Step 1. Begin by placing two of the pieces on top of each other so their rounded ends face opposite directions. Slide the top piece left or right until the large slots on both overlap. You now have a two-layer, miniature craft stick. Do the same for the other two pairs of end pieces.

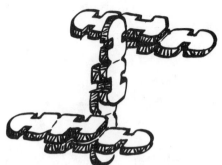

7. Pick up two of the pairs so that their big notches face each other. Give one pair a quarter turn and, you guessed it, snap them together at the big notches. You're now holding a wooden "X" or a big wooden plus sign. The last pair snaps in place in either remaining big notch (your choice). Now there are two pairs next to each other and one at right angles to them in the middle. It helps if the two side-by-side pairs have a matching alignment (stubby side to stubby side and long side to long side) so that they can "lean" on each other when you apply the rubber band.

8. Wrap a rubber band around the center of your paddle wheel to hold it together. It's stronger if you're able to get a wrap in all four corners and four or five twists in all.

9. Slip the paddle wheel inside the rubber band you put on the main part of the boat. This rubber band has to be in two opposite inside corners of the paddle. Most of the wheel should be at or above the sides of the boat. Turn the paddle wheel a few times and then let go. It needs to spin without hitting anything.

10. You're ready to hit the water for a shake-down cruise! Wind up the paddle wheel, place the boat in the water, and let go. You'll have to experiment with the best way to do things. Oh, gee, too bad!

Explanation

There are two main principles involved in this tub toy. One is Newton's Third Law of Motion. In unwinding, the paddle wheel pushes on the water. The water pushes back, moving the boat in the opposite direction. Piece o' cake, huh?

The second principle is transfer of energy. You provide the energy to run this thing by winding up the rubber band. The energy you provided is then stored in the rubber band until you let go. At that point, the energy transfers to the paddle wheel and ultimately shows up again as the motion of the boat. There's lots of energy wasted in this thing, what with water splashing around and such. It's your job to improve things, so, have at it!

Science Fair Suggestions

By controlling variables, you can change all sorts of things on this boat to try and improve its performance. A few suggestions follow.

1. How does the position of the paddle affect the motion of the boat? Before investigating this, you'll have to decide how to evaluate the boat's motion. Should you use speed or distance traveled, or both? Variables to control: the size and shape of the rest of the boat, the number of turns of the paddle to wind it up, the elasticity of the rubber band (remember, this changes over time), how calm the water is (waves affect things), and the amount of wind (if you do it outside).

2. Is the boat's performance affected by how high or low it sits in the water? You could vary this by adding weights to lower it and adding Styrofoam pieces to raise it. Variables to control: basically, the same ones as in number 1.

3. What is the best size and shape of paddle for this boat? This one's a little tricky, because in order to increase the size of the paddle, you also have to increase the size of the boat (otherwise, there's not enough room). So, you could start out with a larger boat and try small and large paddles, but who's to say a small boat with a small paddle isn't better than a large boat with a large paddle? Don't look for answers here! Start experimenting! Variables to control: same as for Steps 1 and 2.

Science Fair Survival Techniques

Activity 8   Precision Pocket Plane

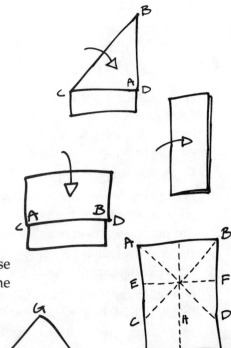

Materials:
    1 sheet of paper
      scissors
      tape

Procedure:

1. Fold point A down to point D. Crease and unfold.

2. Fold point B down to point C. Crease and unfold.

3. Make a hot dog fold (long side to long side). Crease and unfold.

4. Now, fold point A down to point C and point B to point D. Crease and unfold. The fold lines sort of look like a star. You can turn the paper over and refold all the lines if you want.

5. This next step is a little tricky but it's very important. Push a little on the center of the "star" to bring points E and F closer. Pinch E and F together and fold them down to point H. Carefully flatten the paper along the fold lines to form a triangle. Point G is now at the top of the triangle.

6. Fold point G down to point H. Notice that the lower corners of the "roof" (C and D) can be lifted. To keep your plane from acting like a helicopter, either tape these corners down or tuck them under to point H.

7. Turn the plane over and fold it in half along the center crease. Fold the wings downward on both sides as shown. Fold each wingtip upward about a half inch so you have stabilizers.

8. OK, now you're ready to fly! Hold the plane on the underside toward the nose and toss it forward with a flick of your wrist. Outside, your plane will fly long distances in broad loops if there's not too much wind. If the wind is up, throw your plane into the wind pointed slightly upward. Flying the plane inside can be fun if you have a fairly large space to use. Uh, no, the school library is not a good location.

9. Cut four small slits into the backs of the wings for "elevators."

10. Fly the plane under the following conditions:

    a. flaps level
    b. both flaps down
    c. both flaps up
    d. the left flap up and the right flap down
    e. the left flap down and the right flap up

slits

Explanation:

A paper airplane that's angled with its nose upward gets a vertical nudge from the air beneath it as it moves along. Real airplanes rely on Bernoulli's Principle for lift. This law says that stationary (not moving) air can push harder than moving air. This creates a lift for real planes. Your paper model may get *some* help from Mr. Bernoulli, but it's certainly not the sustaining force here that it is for a jumbo jet.

When the "flaps" on your airplane are up, they cause the plane to rotate to a position where it is angled up and gets lift from the air in front of it. Usually, that means straight and level movement until gravity and friction with the air have their way. By changing the positions of the flaps, you can change the direction of rotation caused by the passing air. This results in upward loops, downward loops, or side-to-side rolls.

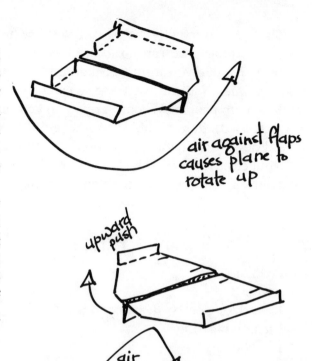

air against flaps causes plane to rotate up

upward push

air flow

Science Fair Suggestions

1. What material is best for keeping this plane in the air the longest? To check this out, you need to make a bunch of planes using different materials, such as notebook paper, construction paper, and typing paper. Variables to control: the size and shape of the plane (tough to do, since you have to make different planes each time), how hard and in what direction you throw the plane (also difficult to control), the position of the flaps, the amount of wind, and how you time the flight.

2. Is there a limit to how many loops a plane can make on one throw? It would seem that the larger you make the flaps, the more loops the plane will make. But at some point, really large flaps might make the whole thing fly about as well as a rock. Variables to control: same as for number 1, but also keep the material the same.

The first two activities below deal with the human body. No, not brain transplants. Shucks. But there are a few things you can do to see how people respond to different situations. The following two experiments give you a little background on measuring the human heartbeat and measuring human reaction time. You can use these to explore some interesting things. One big caution, though, about working with people: Whomever you do your experiment on (be it your little brother, your best friend, or Uncle Fred), they should *always* have the option of stopping the experiment at any time. Also, you should never do anything that could harm your subject either physically or mentally. That obviously rules out electric shocks, highly stressful situations, and verbal abuse. Basically, use common sense and ask yourself if *you* would mind doing the things you're asking your subject to do.

Activity 9   The Pulse and the Pendulum

Materials:
  1 wrist
  1 watch or clock with a second hand
  1 length of string
  1 washer

1. Place your hand over your heart. Feel a beat? If so, you may continue. If not, close this book immediately and back away slowly because *zombies* are not allowed to do these activities.

2. Find your pulse: a) on the underside of your wrist, or b) on the side of your neck under your jaw. Use two fingers of one hand to do this and don't press hard. What you're feeling is blood surging through your arteries with every beat of your heart (Hmmm, sounds like the lead-in to a song.)

3. Sit down with your pencil and paper (no, it's not a test)! Here's where you may need a helper. Count how many times your pulse beats in fifteen seconds, then record your data. Now, do this about five times.

   Sitting: Number of beats in fifteen seconds
   1 _____
   2 _____
   3 _____
   4 _____
   5 _____

4. Now record three trials while you're standing up.

   Standing: Beats in fifteen seconds
   1 _____
   2 _____
   3 _____
   4 _____
   5 _____

5. Now, while you're lying down.

    Lying Down: Number of beats in fifteen seconds

    1 _____

    2 _____

    3 _____

    4 _____

    5 _____

6. Try running in place for about five minutes.

    After Running: Number of beats in fifteen seconds

    1 _____

    2 _____

    3 _____

    4 _____

    5 _____

Explanation

Blood gets to all parts of your body via the circulatory system. It consists of the heart, arteries (carry blood from the heart), veins, and capillaries (iddy-biddy tubes that allow materials to go between your blood and all cells of your body). The heart does a whole bunch of pumping to keep the blood moving. Every pulse you feel is your heart giving your blood another shove. The circulatory system carries all sorts of things to different parts of the body like oxygen, nutrients, and defenders. It carries away yucky stuff like carbon dioxide, waste, and excess water for removal. You're going to concentrate on the "oxygen to" part.

Most people take their pulse and find it varies even when they're just sitting down. Standing up usually causes the pulse to be higher and lying down causes the pulse to be lower. What the heck is going on here? To help you figure it out, make a pendulum by tying a string to a washer, as shown.

Hold the loose end of the string and let the washer hang straight down. This is called the pendulum's equilibrium position (its normal resting position). Pull the washer to the left a little bit and let go. It swings back to and through the equilibrium position and back and forth while it still has the energy you gave it. Eventually, it comes to rest at the equilibrium position. Gravity and friction are causing the pendulum to slow down and finally stop. In a way, these forces are like a sheep dog that herds the pendulum back to its equilibrium position whenever it moves away from it.

Your circulatory system is like a pendulum. It wants to maintain a steady supply of oxygen to all parts of the body, especially your brain. You might say the body's oxygen level has an "equilibrium position." The heartbeat, or pulse, is like the force of gravity acting on the pendulum. The brain is constantly testing the oxygen level of your blood and tries to keep it at the equilibrium position. When you lie down, the heart can keep the same oxygen supply going by beating slower, because it doesn't have to work so hard against gravity. If your heartbeat the same whether you were lying down or sitting up, you'd get too much oxygen when lying down. Standing up, your heartbeat has to increase to keep the same supply of oxygen to the upper part of your body and pull the waste blood from the lower part of your body.

When you run, your muscles require more oxygen and need to get rid of more waste materials. In order to deliver on this demand, the heart has to speed up. The increased demand for oxygen means the lungs have to work faster, too. You might have noticed that your heartbeat went up and down just while you were sitting still. That's because even small changes in position, temperature, or mental state can require different amounts of oxygen and that means changing the heartbeat. All this goes on without you having to think about it. It's handled by the autonomic nervous system.

The most obvious injury you can have to your circulatory system is a cut. The key that you've got a hole in your circulatory system is that blood leaks out! Fortunately, the blood is able to form a clot, which keeps more blood from escaping. Direct pressure on a wound usually helps the clotting process. The exception here is hemophilia (a genetic blood disorder) when blood doesn't clot very well or at all. A second exception is if you cut yourself so badly that the blood is rushing out too fast to clot. You'll want to get to a hospital if this happens. Duh.

The most known of all things that can happen to a circulatory system is a heart attack. A heart attack is caused by the heart muscle not getting enough blood. The arteries in the heart get clogged with junk from an unhealthy life-style. The blood can't get through to the most important muscle of your body and you're in big trouble. Another way blood gets blocked is by a blood clot that forms inside the system. This is serious stuff, because it can block the blood flow to the brain. This is called a stroke, and usually results in some brain damage. A stroke patient can usually recover but may have to relearn many things.

People whose heart can't keep a regular beat can get an artificial pacemaker, which keeps the beat for them. People with messed up arteries or heart valves can get artificial ones, and people with totally messed up hearts can get artificial hearts and heart transplants. Best way to avoid all this is get regular exercise, don't smoke, and eat a variety of good foods. Hey, it's a cinch to take care of yourself!

Extensions

1. Get a thermometer and take your temperature several times during the day. You'll find that your temperature goes up and down, just like your heartbeat. The body does lots of things to keep its temperature at the equilibrium position, such as shivering and sweating. With an adult's help, take the cover off of a thermostat and see how it regulates the room temperature. It works a lot like your body's thermostat.

2. There are many blood borne diseases that affect some people. AIDS is perhaps the best known but least understood. Check with someone who's qualified to help you do research on AIDS and other blood diseases.

3. This might be a great time to set up your own exercise plan. PE at school is fine, but it was never meant to replace your own efforts. Check with an adult and a physician to find out what's best for you. Your body will appreciate it and so will you!

Science Fair Suggestions

1. One way to measure how relaxed or excited a person is is to take their pulse. You might want to find out how various TV programs affect someone's state of relaxation, or see if certain kinds of stories have the same effect on different people. You could also use pulse rate as a lie detector on some people because their pulse increases when they don't tell the truth. Variables to control: the way you take the pulse each time, the body position of the subject, the time of day, the amount of sleep the subject has had, and the amount of stimulants (caffeine from soda pop, sugar, etc.) the person has had.

2. Another type of lie detector measures what is known as galvanic skin response. Basically, you just measure changes in the electrical resistance of someone's skin (this changes as the person sweats) as you ask them questions. There is also an instrument called an ohmmeter which measures resistance between two points on someone's skin. If you can locate an ohmmeter, ask a friend to answer a few questions. Measure his or her pulse rate and see if it corresponds to changes in skin resistance.

Activity 10   The Control Panel

Materials:

3 alligator clips	1 multi-strand wire	friend to assist
1 battery, 9-volt	1 paper clip	water
1 copper wire, insulated, 10" long	1 stick of clay	yard or meter stick
1 flashlight	1 wooden dowel, 10" long	
1 light bulb and socket, 9-volt	½ cup salt	
1 mirror	cup	

Procedure

1. Bend the paper clip into a horseshoe shape so the ends are about one inch apart.

2. Grab (well, at least *ask* first) a friend, brother, sister, aunt, uncle, mother, father, or some other consenting and warm human. Explain that you're going to touch him or her on the arm with either one or two points of the paper clip. The person's job is to tell you how many points you used each time. Have this person turn his or her back to you (or at least close their eyes) and to hold out a bare forearm and hand.

3. Starting at the fingers, touch him or her with two points every time as you move randomly (on both sides) from fingers to hand, to the forearm, and to the elbow. Don't tell your subject whether he or she is right or wrong. Notice patterns, such as places he or she can always tell it's two points and places where he or she has to think about it.

4. Bend the paper clip points till they're about ½ inch apart and try again. The same rules apply. Look for similarities and differences in his responses to touches in the same locations you tested in #3.

5. Now, have your friend turn his or her hand palm down. Using one end of the paper clip, carefully touch the back of his middle finger in different places. Ask him to describe the sensations he feels, like; touch, heat, pain, cold and pressure.

6. Keep that warm blooded person around. Grab the measuring stick.

7. Have your helper hold out his or her hand like you plan to shake it. Hold the measuring stick as shown, with the zero mark on the ruler positioned between his thumb and pointer finger.

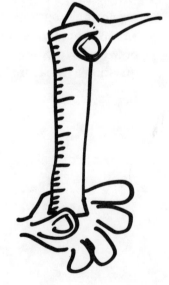

8. Instruct your partner to grab the stick or ruler as soon as you let go. No fair guessing—your partner has to wait until you drop it! Don't give any clues, like saying "1,2,3, . . . Drop!" Let go when you think your partner is *not* ready. Repeat this several times. Each time you do it, record the number on the ruler closest to the top side of your partner's thumb or finger on the same side as your zero mark. What you're doing is measuring how far the ruler or stick drops before your partner is able to react and grab it.

Partner: Distance Dropped

1 _____

2 _____

3 _____

9. Trade places with your partner and repeat the activity on yourself. Same rules, of course!

    You: Distance Dropped

    1 _____

    2 _____

    3 _____

10. Take an average of each person's trials (add 'em up and divide by the number of trials).

    Partner's average: _____   Your average: _____

11. Through the magic of math, you can calculate the **reaction time** (how long it takes your brain to analyze a situation and react to it). Galileo studied the motion of things and found out that everything is pulled toward the Earth at the same rate. In fact, he discovered a relationship between the distance fallen and how long it takes. That relationship is:

    distance fallen = 1/2g(time of fall)^2

    (*g* is a number that's related to the pull of gravity on Earth.)

    If you mess around with the equation a little bit, you can get the "time of fall."

    $$\text{Time of Fall} = \sqrt{\frac{2\,(\text{distance fallen})}{g}}$$

    If you measure your distance in centimeters, the number you put in for g is 980 cm/sec^2. If you measure your distance in inches, the number you put in for g is 384 in/sec^2. After you crunch the numbers, you should get something like 0.5 seconds, or 0.75 seconds, or 1.5 seconds. If you get an answer like 10 seconds, you goofed! It certainly didn't take anyone 10 seconds to grab the measuring stick.

Extensions

1. Lump the modeling clay around one end of the wooden dowel as shown. You're going to use this as a "mallet."

2. Sit down and cross one leg over the other. Let your hanging leg relax. Use the mallet to gently tap your hanging leg just below the knee cap. Keep tapping until you hit the "magic spot." You'll know when you connect because your hanging foot will jerk slightly outward all by itself. This is called a reflex response.

3. Grab a friend and test his or her knee reflex. The taps don't need to be hard, just in the right spot.

Science Fair Survival Techniques

Explanation

Your nervous system gives you input from outside your body — vision, hearing, smell, etc., and inside your body, too — pain, hunger, balance, etc. You analyze and then possibly do something about that input. The nervous system consists of the brain (in your skull), the spinal cord (running down the inside of your backbone), and zillions of nerve cells (also called neurons [néwer-ons]) throughout your body.

The first part of this activity, you started to get an idea of where nerves are concentrated on your hand and arm. Sensitive parts of your body, like your fingers and lips, have nerves close together and near the surface of the skin. That's why your partner could usually tell whether you were poking with one or two points from the paper clip on his fingers. Farther up your arm, the nerves are farther apart and not as near the surface, so you can't as easily tell how many points were used. Fingertips need to be very touch-sensitive, but you usually don't find out how something feels with your forearm.

The nerves on the skin are able to detect five sensations which are: touch, heat, pain, cold and pressure. When the skin is touched, the nerves in the area of contact trigger the different sensations you feel, which are composed of the basic five.

Once your body touches or sees or smells something, what happens next? Think about the reaction time activity. In order to catch the stick, you had to first see it drop. The signal from your eyes had to reach your brain. Your brain had to analyze it and then send a signal to the muscles in your hand to cause your fingers to close and grab the stick. This all took time and explains why you couldn't instantly catch the stick.

The brain doesn't always get involved, though. In a reflex (a muscle movement that happens automatically) like the knee jerk, a signal goes from the place of input (the knee) to the spinal cord, and straight back to the place of input.

Without your brain in the loop, a reflex happens much faster than something that involves lengthy analysis and reaction time. This is usually a good thing. If you touch something very hot, your hand pulls away as a reflex. No sense burning yourself while your brain decides what to do.

OK, great! But how do signals travel around your nervous system? Let's build a model to figure out how this happens. A nerve cell (neuron) looks something like this. It has a cell body or soma, the dendrites, and the axon.

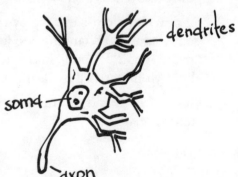

Axons can be very short or very long (some whales have axons over 30 meters long)! The nerve cell gets an electrical signal through the dendrites and chemically sends it thorough the axon to terminal fibrils that pass it on to another nerve cell, or maybe to a bunch of other nerve cells (like your brain), or even to a muscle.

Nerve cells usually don't touch each other. To see how they send signals back and forth, follow the steps below.

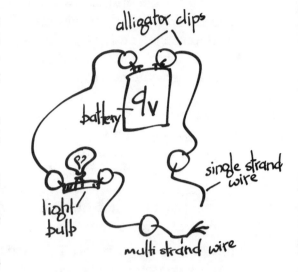

1. Find your multi-strand wire and unwrap and spread about one inch of the wire at one end. This unwrapped, opened end will represent the dendrites of one nerve cell. The single-strand wire you have will represent the axon of a different nerve cell.

2. Connect things as shown in the diagram. Don't touch the multi-strand wire directly to the single-strand wire. You'll fry the light bulb!

3. Put water in the cup and then place your "axon" and "dendrite" in the water on opposite sides of the cup. REMEMBER: Don't let the wires touch or you'll be scrounging another bulb.

   Nothing happens, right? There must be something besides plain water to help carry signals from one nerve cell to another.

4. Remove the wires and pour half of the salt into the water and stir. It helps if the water is warm. Place the wires back in the salt water. There may be some fizzing and a weakly lit bulb. (It helps if you're in a dark room.) If the light doesn't flicker, remove the wires, stir in more salt, and try again. Salt is sodium chloride, NaCl. Sodium and chlorine ions are carrying the electrical flow from one "nerve" to the next. This is similar to what's going on in your body except the chemicals are more than ordinary salt. In your body, the chemicals are known as neurotransmitters.

The nervous system is pretty amazing! Somehow your brain sorts out all the input (that bird chirping, your chair pressing against you, the words you're reading, that itch you want to scratch, etc.) that floods in all at once, figures out what's important, and decides what should be done about it. There's also another very important part of your nervous system — the **autonomic** system [auto-nóm-ik]. This system keeps your heart beating, your food digesting, your lungs moving, your eyes blinking, and much, much more. Basically, the nervous system is responsible for processing everything you feel, sense, learn, and experience from pain to pleasure to happiness to sadness to whatever.

Explanation

The nervous system is responsible for letting us know when some part of our body is not functioning properly or is injured. Neurotransmitters send signals from the affected area to your brain. Certain drugs, such as aspirin, can actually block these sensations by keeping the neurotransmitters from doing their stuff.

Damage to a nerve cell itself can be serious. Unlike bones and ligaments, nerve cells rarely reconnect. This can lead to muscle **atrophy** (few signals get to a muscle, it functions poorly, and wastes away) or even **paralysis** (no signals get through, the muscles don't work at all).

Science Fair Survival Techniques

The nervous system is subject to a variety of problems. Most of them stem from too few signals from the brain, too many all at once, or the wrong signal at the wrong time. You see these as simple occurrences like muscle twitches or as more serious concerns like uncontrolled movement and/or speech. Some of the names may be familiar: epilepsy, cerebral palsy, Parkinson's disease, muscular dystrophy, and multiple sclerosis. As you might expect, nervous system diseases are very serious because nerves don't grow back like other body cells do. There are, however, new medical procedures that can generate nerve growth. Check 'em out!

Extension

1. Investigate your eye reflex. Get a mirror and a flashlight. This is easier to observe if you're in a fairly dark place. Hold the mirror to one eye and the flashlight up to the other. Look at the pupil (the black part) of the eye in the mirror. Turn the flashlight on and off and see what happens to the size of the pupil. This reflex is one way your eyes can protect themselves from bright light.

2. Use the paper clip test on feet and legs, neck and shoulders. You may be surprised at what you find. Try lightly tapping the same point several times to see if sensitivity is lost. Maybe the brain gets tired of keeping track of repetitive input.

3. There are other reflex points on your body similar to the one in your knees. Do some reading to find out where they are and then test them.

Science Fair Suggestions

1. Does a person's reaction time reveal anything about their performance in athletics, schoolwork, or video games? In other words, are some people's nervous systems set up so they have an advantage in certain activities? You could use the dropped ruler to measure reaction times and then find a way to measure performance on different tasks. Variables to control: The time of day, how tired the subjects are, how much and what kind of food the subjects have eaten recently, and how much practice the subjects have had on the various tasks. The last variable will be the most difficult to control. How will you make sure that all subjects have had the same amount of practice on, say, a certain video game? Should you also worry about practice on other video games? (Yes!) One way out of the problem would be to use subjects who have never played a video game in their life, but since that might be impossible, you'll think of other ways to control that variable, won't you?

2. Is there any relation between someone's ability to distinguish between two touches and their reaction time? If so, why should that be so? Variables to control: time of day, how tired the subjects are, how much and what kind of food the subjects have eaten, who drops the ruler each time, and how the ruler is dropped.

3. How can you test the reaction time of a pet, such as the family dog? Dogs are notoriously lousy at catching rulers, so you'd have to come up with something new. Once you've figured that out, you should figure out why anyone would want to know a dog's reaction time.

The next activity involves growing bacteria, molds, and fungi. In other words, really cool, gross stuff. Before doing this as a science fair project, check to see that your school allows experiments where critters are growing.

Activity 11   Invisible Invaders

Materials:

1 petri dish	invisible organisms
agar	liquid disinfectant
bagel or roll	sugar
chlorine bleach	time
clear food wrap	vinegar
gum	water

Procedure:

There are some important things to remember here.

A) Keep things clean.

B) Allow enough time.

C) Take good notes.

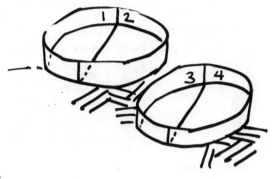

1. Use a marker to draw a line on the outside of both pieces of the petri dish so that each one is divided in half by the line. Also on the outside, number each section.

2. Wash them in hot water and soap (no need to use the dishwasher). Keep the pieces covered and clean after washing. Try not to touch them too much.

3. Stir about one-fourth teaspoon agar into about one-fourth cup water. Bring this mixture to a boil (you may need help for this) and remove it from the heat.

4. Sprinkle in some sugar, if you wish, and stir. (Note: You can speed the clean up and reuse of your dishes by lining them with clear wrap.)

5. Divide this hot mixture between the clean halves of the petri dish (15-20 mls each) and cover each snugly with the clear wrap. Allow time to cool and gel.

6. You now have four test areas in two containers (other small, shallow dishes work, too). There are lots of ways to use these things to grow critters. Keep careful notes of what you do in each section because it may be several days before you begin to see much.

Plan ahead and do both activities for one dish at the same time so you can cover the dish and avoid disturbing it for a week or two (overnight in some cases). Here's where good note taking comes in handy! Draw a picture and write down a description of what you did in each test section.

© 1997 Rev 1999 The Wild Goose Co.

Test Section 1: After a busy play day, use any finger and simply touch one end of the section. Roll your finger slightly on the agar. Now, thoroughly wash your hands and use the same finger to touch the other end of *Section 1*.

Test Section 2: Chew a piece of gum for a long time. Using a clean cotton swab, touch the gum and then draw a "squiggle" on one end of the section. Use **the other end of the swab** and test a friend's gum, a pet's water dish or aquarium, or under a fingernail and draw a squiggle on the *other* end of section 2.

Cover this dish with the wrap again and put it in a dark corner out of sunlight. You can check your dish now and then but don't take the wrap off until there are lots of "things" growing on the agar.

Test Section 3: You'll need a small, fresh piece of bagel, roll, or bread made with no preservatives. Put a drop of water on the sample and place it in section 3.

Test Section 4: Use a two inch piece of sticky tape for this test. Find a spot where many hands have been: a door knob, a faucet handle, the same towel, or a railing. Touch the tape to the surface two or three times but use only the one surface. Next, touch the tape to the gel once or twice. In spots on the gel where the tape touched, put a drop each of chlorine bleach, vinegar, and a liquid disinfectant. Also, use a cotton swab to squiggle a small amount of an antibiotic cream. Cover the dish and put it away the same way you did with the first one. Same rules apply.

Explanation:

The bacteria, molds, and fungi that are growing in your dish are huge groups of living critters that surround us all the time but are usually unseen. You've brought millions and millions of them together for your agar stew and they are seen very easily.

Test Section 1 probably is no surprise to you! There are bacteria on both spots you touched but probably much less on the spot touched after the hand washing. Hmmm, seems all those adults are right: "Wash your hands!" Soap and water remove a huge quantity of microscopic goobers and it's so easy to do.

The squiggles in Test Section 2 are the paths of the swab as it crossed the agar. You tested your spit and perhaps someone else's to see what was there and something certainly was! It's usually a mixture of bacteria and fungi and you probably have lots of both.

Molds and fungi come in a variety of colors, shapes, and smells. Take a close look at Test Section 3 and you'll see many different kinds of mold and fungus. Each little plant makes millions of spores that are floating around us all the time. A spore lands on a bagel (or bread) and takes up residence. If the conditions are right, it grows like crazy and spreads across the surface (and inside) of the bagel. Moldy bagels are evidence that this process is at work all the time!

Test Section 4 probably has some holes and gaps in it. The bacteria you snagged from the door knob (or wherever) can't survive the bleach, disinfectant, and creams. It makes sense to use these things if you want to get rid of as many bacteria as possible so there are fewer chances of getting sick.

Science Fair Suggestions

This activity could serve as a project as it stands, but where's the fun in that? Check out the suggestions below.

1. What brand of disinfectant is most effective in getting rid of bacteria, molds, and fungi? Answering this question involves expanding what you did in Test Section 4. Get a bunch of petri dishes and agar, and grow different kinds of yucky things in each one. Before allowing them to grow, place drops of different disinfectants in different sections of each dish, making sure you keep track of what goes where. Variables to control: amount of disinfectant placed in each dish, temperature of the dishes, exposure of dishes to light, and exposure of dishes to air.

2. How does temperature affect the growth of bacteria and other yucky stuff? Vary the temperature by placing different petri dishes in different environments (next to a heater, in a refrigerator, in a freezer, etc.). Variables to control: exposure to light, the manner in which the dishes are contaminated with bacteria (this affects how much you have in the dish in the first place), and the amount of agar in the dishes.

The following set of experiments use water to push things, move things, make pretty bubbles, and measure time. Bet you didn't know water was so versatile!

Activity 12   Hero's Engine

Materials

2 pipettes	scissors
1 length of string, 24"	tape
1 Styrofoam cup	thread
petroleum jelly or modeling clay	water

Procedure

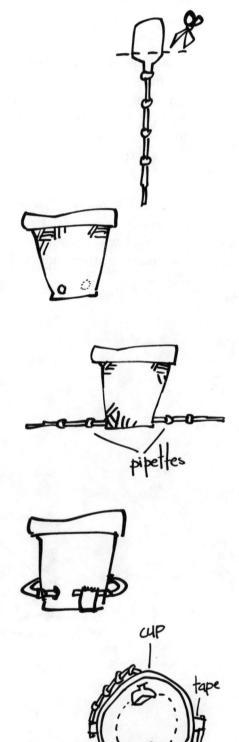

1. Look at the directions carefully on this one. It's a little tricky. Cut two-thirds of the bulb end from each pipette.

2. Poke small holes on opposite sides near the bottom of the Styrofoam cup.

3. Push the pipettes through these holes from the inside out until the bulb part of the pipette is snug against the side of the cup.

4. Fill the cup with water and make sure the water flows out of the cup through the two pipettes. No, that's not all you're going to do. You're checking to see that water doesn't leak from the holes in the cup rather than going through the pipettes. If you have a leak, try to make the pipettes fit more snugly or try to patch the leaks with modeling clay, petroleum jelly, or start over with a new Styrofoam cup.

pipettes

5. Now comes the hard part. Take a piece of tape, about six inches long, and wrap one end around the small end of a pipette. Gently bend the pipette toward the cup until you can attach the free end of the tape to the side or bottom of the cup. Make sure the pipette doesn't get any kinks in it when you bend it.

6. Do the same with the other pipette, bending it so that it makes an "S" shape that follows rather than meets the other pipette.

7. Carefully poke two holes in the top edge of the cup on opposite sides. Lace about a ten-inch length of string through the holes and tie it so you've given your cup a long handle. Tie a short length of thread (about 3 inches) in the middle of the string handle so that the cup hangs straight and level when you hold the thread.

cup

tape

8. Fill the cup with water, hold it by the thread, and watch what happens. Don't do this at the dinner table.

pipette

Explanation

The secret to understanding Hero's engine lies in a neat principle that's known as Newton's Third Law. You might have heard it called action and reaction. It's a simple but interesting fact that when you push on something, the something pushes back. If you push on a wall, the wall pushes back. If you throw a rock, the rock pushes back until it leaves your hand.

Because of the downward force of gravity, the water inside the Styrofoam cup shoots out the ends of the pipettes. Wanting to obey Newton's Third Law (It really doesn't have a choice), the water pushes back on the pipettes. The energy from that push is transferred to the cup, causing the cup to spin on the string.

Science Fair Suggestions

1. How can you make the cup spin as fast as possible? Before tackling this question, you'll have to figure out a neat way to determine how fast the cup is spinning. Once you've solved that problem, you can perform lots of mini-experiments, changing only one variable in each experiment. For example, you could find out how the diameter of the cup affects spinning speed. Variables to control: amount of water in the cup, material the cup is made from, location and orientation of the pipettes, and the number of pipettes.

2. You'll notice that the cup spins slower as more and more water leaves the cup. That's because there's less and less water in the cup pushing down, which makes the water come out of the pipettes slower. Slower water means less of a push back on the cup. Is there a way to put together a hero's engine so the spinning speed is constant? Check out the following activities on water clocks for a few hints.

In the next two activities, you'll build clocks that use dripping water to measure time. It's suggested that you try both of them first, before using them as the basis for a science fair project.

Activity 13   Liquid Time

Materials

1 bottle cap (from an 8 oz. bottle)	1 plastic bottle, 8 oz.
1 clear plastic cup, 2 oz.	1 push pin
1 handy, dandy clock	1 ruler
1 large cereal bowl	1 sharpened pencil
1 marker	paper clips
1 pair of scissors	water

Procedure I

1. Remove the inner lining from the cap that goes on the 8 oz. bottle (any plastic bottle that looks like the one in the diagram can be used; an old empty shampoo bottle works great). Use the push pin to poke a <u>small</u> hole in the center of the cap. **Don't** push the pin all the way through. Push it through just enough so you can see a very tiny hole. Oh yeah, be careful not to poke a hole in your finger as well.

2. Fill the bowl about three-fourths full of water and place the cap, upside down, on the water so that it floats. Add paper clips to the inside of the cap until water starts to seep into the hole. Do this several times and watch your handy clock to see if it takes about the same amount of time for the cap to sink.

Explanation

Believe it or not, what you've just built is a water clock. If you play with it a bit, you'll find that the cap takes about the same amount of time each trial to fill up with water and sink. The very first water clocks used metal or clay bowls instead of plastic caps because plastic wasn't invented yet! The Greeks called these clocks **clepsydras** (klé-psidra), which is a word that means "water thief." It hasn't been determined just who they thought was stealing water. The clepsydra you built is probably more trouble than it's worth, because to record long periods of time you have to keep emptying the plastic cap and starting over. In the next section, you'll build a new and improved clepsydra.

Procedure II

1. Ask an adult for help and cut just the bottom off the 8-ounce plastic bottle.

2. Use the push pin to make four vent holes in the side of the clear plastic cup. Place the holes so they are three-fourths inch from the cup bottom and 1¼ inches apart around the circumference of the cup.

3. Remove the cap from the bottle and turn the clear, plastic cup upside down. Position the bottle top onto the bottom *center* of the clear, plastic cup bottom. Trace around the bottle rim so that you now have a circle on the bottom center of the clear, plastic cup (see the diagram). Cut a hole in the *bottom* of the cup by using the circle you drew as a guide. Don't worry if you slip up a bit when cutting the hole, because it doesn't have to be exact.

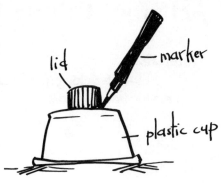

4. Screw the neck of the bottle through the hole in the cup so that the neck is inside the cup. Take the cap with the tiny hole (you made above) and screw it onto the bottle neck. If you put everything together correctly, the cup should now serve as a base so you can stand the bottle upside down. Check the diagram.

5. Go to the sink and fill the upside down bottle with water and set it down so that it drains into the sink. Notice how fast the water comes out of the hole in the cap. If it's a steady *drip*, you're in business. If it's a steady *stream* of water, pick up another cap and use the push pin to poke a smaller hole in the center. Put the bottle where the dripping water won't damage anything.

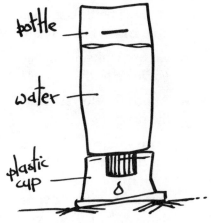

6. What you've just built is another simple water clock. You can use this clock to measure time based on the water level in the bottle. Make a mark on the outside, about an inch from the top of the clock (formerly the bottom of the bottle). Fill the bottle up to this mark. As the water drips out of the clock, mark the water level every minute. If you've got a really slow-dripping clock, mark the water level every five minutes.

7. When you're done, look at the pattern of marks. Are they evenly spaced? If not, what's the pattern?

More Explanation

Water clocks were probably first developed by the Egyptians as early as 1500 B.C. They have been modified throughout the years by people in different countries. The second water clock you made is better than the first in several ways. First, you can time several one minute or five-minute periods in a row just by watching as the water level drips past separate marks or as the index card wheel turns. Only one segment of time can be measured by your sinking cup or sand timer. Once the cup sinks or the sand runs out, you have to start again. Another problem with this first type of clock is that it needs to be reset all the time, after all, containers can't fill themselves with water.

Finally, you can do cool things with dripping water and changing water levels that you can't do with sinking bowls. Dripping water can turn water wheels, which can turn other wheels and make things move. Changing water levels can also cause things to turn and move if you're clever enough to put the right gears together.

There is one problem with the Greek water clock you just built. You probably noticed that the marks on the side of the bottle got closer and closer together as the water level dropped. That's because the weight of the water in the bottle is what pushes the water at the base out the bottom hole. As the water level goes down, there's less water above pushing the water out the bottom, therefore it doesn't drip as fast.

Science Fair Survival Techniques

Activity 14   Drip Time

Materials
1 Greek water clock (previous activity)	1 pair of scissors
3 plastic bottles, 2 oz.	1 push pin
1 clear plastic cup	clear tape
1 marker	water

Procedure

1. Put a piece of tape over the hole in the cap of the Greek water clock you just made. Set the bottle/cup combo aside for a minute.

2. Cut the very bottoms off all three of the 2 oz. plastic bottles. Use the push pin to poke tiny holes in all three bottle caps, just as you did for the previous water clock. Remember you can always make a hole larger, but it's hard to make it smaller!

3. Go to a sink and fill each small bottle with water. Figure out which one drips the fastest and which bottle drips the slowest. You might want to mark which is which so you don't lose track.

4. Attach the slowest-dripping 2 oz. bottle to the clear plastic cup, just as you did for the 8 oz. bottle in the previous activity.

5. Once secured, take scissors and snip the plastic cup from top to bottom on two opposite sides. Don't cut the flat bottom of the plastic cup, only the two sides. Place the snipped cup and 2 oz. bottle contraption over the 8 oz. bottle (former Greek clock). Push the sides of the plastic cup together so that it fits snugly over the 8 oz. bottle. When you get a good fit, tape the sides of the plastic cup in that position. Remove the taped cup/2 oz. bottle contraption

6. Fill the 2 oz. bottle, that is attached to the taped cup, with water. Grab the next slowest 2 oz. bottle, turn it upside down and place it on top of the first one. Fill that bottle with water and then place the last and fastest dripping 2 oz. bottle on top of that bottle. Fill the third bottle with water and now you're ready to save time with some bottles.

7. Using the push pin, poke a couple of holes into the sides of the bottom two bottles. Put the holes just below where the cap from the above bottle reaches. After you've done this, watch water drip for awhile as you continuously fill the top bottle with water. Check that the water level in the bottom bottle stays the same as water drips out.

8. Place this whole contraption on top of the 8 oz. bottle so that water from the small bottles drip and gradually fill it. When you're done, you should have something that looks like the drawing.

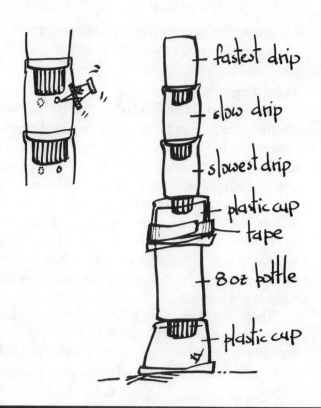

fastest drip
slow drip
slowest drip
plastic cup
tape
8 oz bottle
plastic cup

9. Watch for awhile again, making sure that the water level in the bottom small bottle remains the same. If everything seems to be working okay, start everything over. This time mark the water level in the large bottle every minute or every five minutes for a slow drip. Use a marker to mark the outside of the bottle. As the top small bottle empties, keep it filled with fresh water.

10. As the large bottle fills, check out the pattern of your marks. Are they evenly spaced or does the spacing change?

Explanation

Okay, if everything went as planned, the marks on the side of the large bottle should have been evenly spaced, meaning that the water came out of the small bottles at a constant rate. By setting things up the way you did, you made sure the water level in the bottom small bottle was always the same. Therefore, as time passed, the water came out at the same rate. As a side note, the reason you poked holes in the sides of the small bottles was that air pressure in and outside the bottles would have messed up your entire clock. The holes prevented air pressure from being a problem.

The Chinese didn't use plastic bottles for their clocks. Duh. They used a series of large containers that were stacked on top of one another, and of course they were decorated with all sorts of cool stuff. A lot more complicated than the clock in your living room and probably a little fancier, too. The one problem with these clocks was that you had to keep hauling water and filling them up.

Science Fair Suggestions

Now that you've done these two activities, you know something about how water clocks work. If you're up for a real challenge, you could do your best to build the most accurate and reliable water clock you can. For example, you could use a series of large plastic bowls instead of the plastic bottles. Of course, you'd have to figure out how to support the bowls so one drips into another. You could also experiment with liquids other than water. While you're at it, why not figure out a way for the water supply in your clock to replenish itself? Some kind of pump should do the trick, but you don't want to pump too fast or too slow. Talk to the folks at your local plumbing supply or at the fish store. To make your efforts scientific you'll have to control variables, just as with all the other experiments. That means change only one thing at a time as you're developing the best water clock ever.

© 1997 Rev 1999 The Wild Goose Co.

Activity 15 Magic Circles and Square Bubbles

Materials

1 bottle of glycerin	liquid dish soap	tape
copper wire	pipe cleaners	thread
large bowl	pliers	water

Procedure

1. Bend the wire so it forms a three-inch loop with a handle like a big lollipop. The loop doesn't have to be perfect but it needs to be fairly smooth. You have to wrap the end of the wire securely so there's no way it can come apart or have a point that will pop your soap film. Use the pliers and then wrap the joint with tape if you need to cover edges.

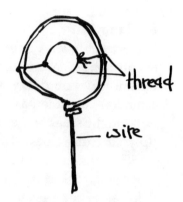

2. Do these next steps when you're feeling patient. This takes a little time, but it's worth it. Cut a six-inch length of thread and tie a loop in it. Leave a two-inch tail of excess thread. The thread loop is about one inch and should be much smaller than the wire loop.

3. Tie the tail of the thread to the wire loop, so that the thread loop is in the middle of the wire loop.

4. Cut another piece of thread and use it to tie the free side of the thread loop to the closest side of the wire loop. You should end up with something like the picture, though the thread loop my not look like a perfect circle.

5. Time to mix some bubble solution. Open your glycerine and add half a capful (3.5mls) to a large bowl or stoppered sink. Now add five cups of water (1.2L) and a half a cup (118 mls) of liquid dish soap. Stir it up, and you're ready to make bubbles.

6. Dip your "double lollipop" into the bubble solution. When you lift it out, everything inside the wire loop should have soap film on it. If not, try again. Then, create a bubble.

7. Now for the magic part: pop the film that's *inside* the thread loop. This effect is caused by surface tension in the bubble solution. See if you can figure out what's going on before you read the explanation. Do this as much as you want because it's just plain cool!

8. Use some wire or pipe cleaners to make a cube. If you're clever about bending the wire, you can make most of the cube by bending the wire at right angles. You may have to cut at least three extra lengths of wire, though. Make sure the cube is small enough to be completely submerged in the bubble solution. See the diagram.

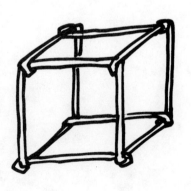

9. Dunk your cube into the bubble solution and remove it. Zowie! Try this several times to create different bubble designs. Try popping one or two sides of your soap film and see what happens.

Explanation

Soap molecules have their own brand of surface tension that's different from water. Soap molecules form long chains so they're better suited for making thin films, as in bubbles. Soap molecules like each other and they also like things like thread and wire. They easily latch onto each other as well as the thread and wire.

In the magic ring activity, the thread formed a perfect circle after you popped the "bubble" inside. That's because the soap molecules between the thread and the wire all pulled outward on the thread evenly in all directions. This same sort of thing is what makes the soap bubbles you blow always form into spheres.

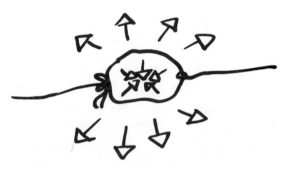

The shape of your film is sometimes determined by what's holding it. The neat designs you got with your wire cube are examples of soap films from different sides of the cube getting together. Because soap molecules chain together, the shape of the wire on the outside has an effect on the shape of the soap film on the inside but it may be very different from what you might expect. The way Mother Nature does it is to use the shortest, strongest structure to save energy and effort.

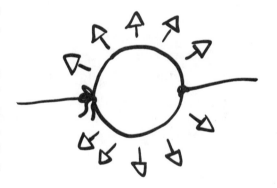

Extensions

1. Try bending the wire into different shapes, such as pyramids and spirals. Dip these into your bubble solution. Make sure you don't have any pointy wire ends sticking out. Soap films need closed loops to form.

2. Dip a finger in the bubble solution. Make some cool wire bubbles and show your friends how you can poke your finger through the films without popping them. Encourage your friends to try (make sure their fingers are dry) and watch the films pop. While basking in your superiority, see if you can figure out why soap-covered fingers don't pop the films.

Science Fair Survival Techniques

Science Fair Suggestions

1. What bubble solution recipe gives you the longest-lasting bubbles? To answer this question, you might be tempted to just mix up a bunch of different kinds of batches and try them out. A more scientific approach, though, requires some careful planning. For starters, let's keep the amounts of water and liquid soap constant at five cups of water and a half cup of soap. Then vary the amount of glycerin added from ¼ capful to half a capful to ¾ capful to 1 capful. The next step would be to change the amount of water to, say, 5½ cups while keeping the soap at half a cup, and again varying the amount of glycerin from ¼ capful to 1 capful. Then each time you change the water amount, you have to check it with all four amounts of glycerin. If you check out four different amounts for each of the liquids (water, soap, and glycerin), there are 64 possible combinations! Maybe you should start with just three different amounts of each liquid!

2. Does the size of the cube or pyramid (or whatever!) affect the kind of bubbles that are formed? To answer this, just make some wire shapes that are different sizes and see what happens. Variables to control: Material the shapes are made from, the recipe for the bubble solution, how long you dip the shapes in the solution, how you hold the shapes as you pull them out of the solution, and how fast you pull the shapes out of the solution.

Activity 16 Monsoon Measure

Materials
- 2 push pins
- 1 craft stick
- 1 hair dryer
- 1 human hair
- 1 index card
- 1 paper tube
- 1 shower or sink
  - clear tape

Procedure

1. Pull out a human hair that's about 6 inches long. If you have a buzz cut, find a friend who's willing to donate a hair to science.

2. Grab your craft stick and push pin. Take the push pin and drill a hole in the center of both ends of the craft stick about ¼" from the tip.

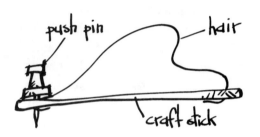

3. Pull the hair through one end of the craft stick. Fold the hair around the stick near the hole and tape it in place.

4. Take a push pin and stick it through the hole that you just used for the hair. Run the other end of the hair through the hole in the opposite end of the craft stick, but do not attach it.

5. Stand the paper tube on end. Take the push-pin and craft stick combo and shove the push pin through the paper tube about 1 inch from the bottom. Glance at the diagram and move on.

6. Grab the other push pin and push it into the paper tube about 1 inch from the top. Make sure that it's directly in line with the bottom push pin.

7. Line up the bottom of the index card with the bottom of the paper tube. Tape the index card (with the plain side facing you) lengthwise to the back side of the paper tube. The index card should extend to the right like a flag on a flagpole. If you need some help, check the drawing on the next page.

8. Gently loop the dangling hair over the top push pin. You can adjust the tension on the hair by pulling on the end that is threaded through the hole in the craft stick but not attached. Position the craft stick so that it is level and perpendicular to the paper tube. The tip of the craft stick should point towards the index card.

9. Once you position the craft stick correctly, <u>do</u> <u>not</u> adjust the hair anymore. Carefully fold the end of the hair you are holding around the craft stick and tape it in place. On the attached index card, mark the position of the end of the craft stick.

10. The tool you just built is called a **hygrometer** (hygro + meter) and it measures moisture in the air, so let's test it. Place your hygrometer in a bathroom, turn on the shower or sink, and close the door. After about two minutes, turn off the water and close the door again. After about ten minutes, check your hygrometer for changes. The position of the end of the craft stick should have changed. Compare it with the first mark you made. Move your hygrometer out of the bathroom and observe any changes.

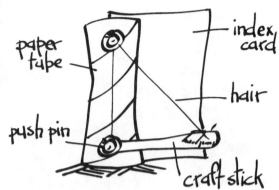

11. Turn a hair dryer on your hygrometer for awhile. Use a no-heat setting if possible. Note any changes in the position of the end of the craft stick. After that, remove the hair dryer and see if your hygrometer returns to its original condition.

Explanation

Believe it or not, all your everyday, garden-variety air has water in it. It's in the form of **water vapor**, which is just a bunch of individual water molecules. Weather people use the term **humidity** to describe how much water is in the air. 5% humidity means there's not much water in the air and the air actually feels dry. In contrast, 95% humidity means there's so much water in the air that breathing feels like sucking on a sponge. Think about a typical summer day. How hot and sticky it is outside depends on the humidity level and the level of humidity depends on where you live. Mountain and desert areas usually have low humidity, while locations near the ocean usually have high humidity.

The hair and craft stick portion of your hygrometer is able to detect small differences in humidity. When there's more water in the air, the hair absorbs it and actually gets a bit longer. That's why the end of the craft stick moves down when you place it in a bathroom with the water running. When there's not as much water in the air, water in the hair evaporates and the hair shortens, causing the end of the craft stick to move up.

Humidity makes a big difference in the weather. For one thing, if there's very little water in the air, you're probably not going to get a big rainstorm. You may be wondering how humidity affects you. Think *summer*. When the temperature is high, one way you cool off is to sweat. The sweat evaporates from your skin, taking heat with it, and that makes you feel cooler. However, if the air is really humid, and contains lots of water vapor, it's much more difficult for the sweat to evaporate. The result is wet, sticky skin, but you don't feel any cooler. On the other hand, if there's little humidity in the air, sweat evaporates quickly and you feel much cooler. That explains why you may *feel* more comfortable with a temperature of 110 degrees in Phoenix, Arizona where there's low humidity than you might at 95 degrees in New Orleans, Louisiana where there's high humidity. For most people, 110 degrees is <u>hot</u> no matter what the humidity.

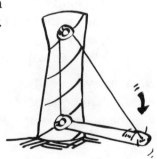

Extension Ideas

    Find a sheltered spot outside for your hygrometer and check it daily. Try calibrating your hygrometer by reviewing the newspaper's daily weather report. You can also watch your favorite TV meteorologist and learn a lot about the weather in your area. Most weathercasters will give you the current temperature outside and at least one humidity reading. Write down that information and go check your hygrometer. When the craft stick moves on your hygrometer, make a corresponding mark on the index card. The marks will show you the percentage of humidity in the air.

Science Fair Suggestions

1. Does the kind of hair used affect the performance of the hygrometer? See how the device works with various shades of blond, brown, and brunette hair. Variables to control: length of the hair, where the hygrometer is placed, and the range of humidity you test. This last one is very difficult to control, because turning on the shower for 5 minutes won't always give you the same humidity. You almost need a commercial hygrometer to check the humidity level.

2. Are there other substances besides human hair that will work in your hygrometer? You could test string, thread, dog hair, yarn, and fishing line. Variables to control: same as for Step 1.

On Your Own

On Your Own

By the time you reach this section of the book, you've either gone through the first two sections or you have a pretty good idea how to go about doing a science fair projects. 'Cause what's here is a large collection of activities that are designed to get your brainwaves cooking so you can come up with a project on your own. If these activities don't get you started, you might want to spend a little more time on the previous section of the book, where there is a little more help available.

Classic Guitar

Materials
16 notched craft sticks
3 large rubber bands
2 small rubber bands
1 box with lid (about the size of a shoe box or cereal box)
1 friend
1 pair of scissors
1 sharp knife
1 soup can, 15 oz.
1 square of paper, 4"

Procedure

1. Take a good look at one of the notched craft sticks and notice that there are four places where the stick is "scored." What that means is that if you hold the stick lengthwise there are four distinct vertical lines on the stick. By snapping the craft stick at these spots, you can easily break it into different sized pieces and that's just what you're about to do. Look carefully at the next couple drawings so that you can become "one" with the craft stick.

2. To get the **long pieces** you need, take a craft stick and break off two scored sections on one end. Look at the illustration and if it matches your stick, do nine more sticks just like it. You should now have a total of <u>ten</u> large size sticks.

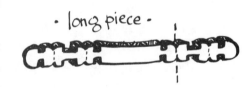

3. To get the **middle pieces** you need, take a craft stick and break off all four scored sections just like the drawing. Once again, if your stick matches the drawing, make five more of the same. You should now have a total of <u>six</u> middle size sticks.

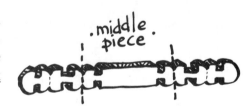

4. Good job so far! Now you need some **small** segments. Pick up any of the pieces you broke off from the other sticks. What you want are the smallest sections of the stick (about ¾" long). If you haven't broken off all the scored segments, do it now. Keep <u>two</u> of the little segments that have the widest indentations on the side. These segments look like mini barbells or dog bones. In addition, save <u>four</u> of the small segments that have rounded tops (they are the original end pieces of the craft sticks) The drawing will guide you.

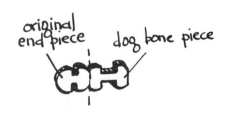

5. Take all your sticks and put the matching ones in separate piles.

Science Fair Survival Techniques

6. Grab one long piece and hold it in your hand so that the flat side of the stick is facing you and the rounded portion is pointing up.

7. Take one of the small rounded segments from the pile of four. Slip it into the second slot down from the top on the right side of the stick as it faces you. Make sure the rounded end of the small segment is facing you. By all means check the drawing.

8. Grab one middle-sized stick out of the pile of six and fit it into the same slot, on top of the small segment you just positioned. Like the small segment, it should be perpendicular to the stick in your hand and the long part should be aimed towards you.

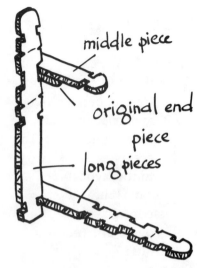

middle piece

original end piece

long pieces

9. Take another one of the long pieces and fit it into the bottom slot of the craft stick you're holding so that the long portion with the rounded-end is pointed at you. One more look at the drawing will help.

10. Reach down and pick up another long stick. Slide it next to the first stick you're holding, so that it fits over the perpendicular sticks and the flat side is facing you. The drawing my dears, check the drawing.

11. Position three perpendicular sticks on the right side of the long stick you just added. Make sure the sticks are in exactly the same configuration as steps 6-9. Now slide a third long stick up against the other two you are holding. Take a small rubber band and go over and around the bottom of the two long sticks so that they are secured to the three flat sticks. Wow, that wasn't easy but you finished the first step! The drawing will show you what you did.

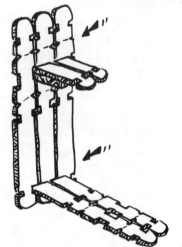

12. Repeat what you just did and make another notched stick contraption that looks exactly like the first one.

13. Get the box. The box is about to become the body of your guitar. If there's a lid to the box, tape it on. Hold the box vertically with one of the large flat sides of the box facing you. Measure 3½" from the top of the box and make a mark. Now measure about 2" from the bottom and make a mark. Make a circle that's 3" in diameter between these two marks. The easiest way is to find a 15-oz. soup can, set it down between your two marks and trace around it.

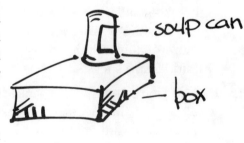

soup can

box

14. Use scissors or a sharp knife to cut the circle out of your box. You should probably get an adult to help you. Remember not to bend the box while you're cutting the hole.

15. Hold the box vertically so that the short sides are pointing up and down. Clip a craft stick device to the center of both short box sides. Make sure the long stick portions are on the back of the box (not the side with the hole). On the side with the hole, both small rounded sticks should fit snugly under the top edge of the box. The two middle sticks will lay flat on the front (hole side) of the box. On the back of the box, loop a large rubber band over the two lips created by the craft stick structures on either end. This is a tough step, so take a good long look at the drawing.

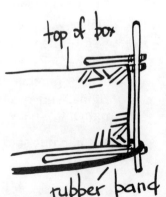

top of box

rubber band

16. To position the guitar strings (rubber bands) correctly, loop each rubber band around the ends of both craft stick devices on either side of the hole. Both rubber bands should loop around two adjoining sticks and fit in the bottom slot of the craft stick devices. Once again, look closely at the diagram.

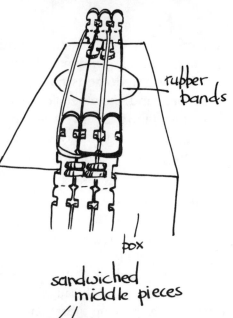

rubber bands

box

17. Congrats! You finished the main body of your guitar. All you have to build now is the **bridge**. Take the last two middle pieces you have left and sandwich them together. Fit them into the two small "dog bone" pieces. In other words, there should be a "bone" on either end of the two sandwiched pieces. Take a peek at the drawing.

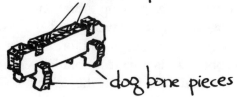

sandwiched middle pieces

18. Ask an adult to help you with this next step. You need to use a sharp knife to carve two extra notches in the bridge between the notches that already exist. The notches should be evenly spaced apart. Check the drawing for this step.

dog bone pieces

19. Place the bridge on the guitar, underneath the rubber band strings by the end nearest the hole in the box. The drawing will help you with proper placement.

20. Okay, you're ready to do a screaming guitar solo! First, strum the guitar a little bit and see how it sounds. Most likely it will be out of tune, but don't worry about that right now. You're going to try some other things first.

cut here

21. Place the 4-inch square of paper over the hole in the box. Make sure that the paper doesn't touch the rubber band strings. See how that changes the sound.

22. Now, leave the hole uncovered and pluck one of the "strings" of your guitar. Move the bridge either toward or away from the hole and pluck again. What happens to the sound? Try this using all possible positions of the bridge (from the hole all the way to the edge of the box). Consider the following ideas: What sound changes occur as you move the bridge closer to the hole? What sound changes occur as you move the bridge closer to the edge of the box?

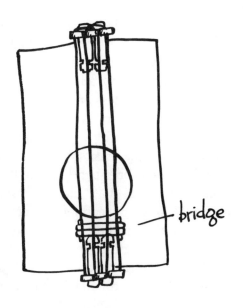

23. You can adjust how tight each rubber band string is by how many times you wrap it around the three craft sticks on either side of the guitar hole. By stretching or relaxing the rubber band strings, you change the sound of the strings. Listen carefully to the plucked sound as you adjust the strings. What sounds do you get as the rubber band strings gets tighter? What sounds do looser strings make?

bridge

Science Fair Survival Techniques

24. Experiment with the strings until you can either play a tune by plucking individual strings or you can get a cool sound by strumming all the strings together. Try moving the bridge around. Basically what you're doing is tuning your guitar. It won't be easy because as you tighten one side of the rubber band, the other side tends to get looser. Take your time and sooner or later you'll get a sound that isn't too bad. If you get a pretty decent strum, don't rush out and practice stage diving. No need to get an agent yet. As a matter of fact, before you try getting a gig as the opening act for some major band, you may want to try a little more practice.

Explanation

Now that you've been playing some pretty intense riffs on your guitar, let's talk a little bit about music. There are many different kinds of music but all music has one thing in common and that is that all music is sound. The question now becomes, what is sound? Well, to understand sound, you must first take a quick look at air. Air is made up of zillions of tiny particles called molecules. As molecules move around, they naturally bump into things like your eardrum. Your eardrums are kind of like little receivers that pick up vibrations caused by moving air molecules. Anything that makes air molecules move around can cause sound. For example, the rubber band strings you plucked on your guitar created

sound and that back and forth movement of the rubber bands is called vibration. The larger the vibration, the larger the sound. Grab your guitar and pluck one of the rubber bands really hard. Watch the rubber band closely and notice that as the sound dies down, the vibration of the rubber band gets smaller and smaller.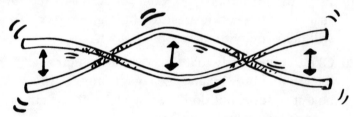

You probably noticed that the sound of the guitar is much louder and richer when the hole in the box is uncovered instead of covered. That's because when you vibrate one of the strings, the box also vibrates and that in turn creates sound waves inside the box. When the hole is uncovered, you can hear the sound waves in the box better and everything is louder. This explains why some guitars are so expensive. There is a real art to making a guitar body (box) that vibrates to produce rich, beautiful sound.

In addition to discovering how loud your guitar can play, you also investigated what made the sound of your guitar higher or lower. Pitch is the technical word for how high or low a note plays. You were able to change the pitch of your rubber band strings in two ways.

One way was by adjusting the length of the vibrating rubber band and the other way was by adjusting the tightness or tension. You were able to change the length of the rubber bands by changing the position of the bridge. Only the part of the rubber band that's between the bridge and the opposite end of the box actually vibrates and the shorter the rubber band length, the higher the pitch. You were able to modify the tension by stretching or relaxing the rubber band. What you probably noticed is that the tighter the rubber band, the higher the pitch. On a real guitar, you adjust the tension by turning the small tuning pegs that hold the strings in place. You alter the length of the strings by pushing them against the small raised metal pieces on the neck of the guitar called frets.

One more thing before you try a couple experiments with your guitar. You may be wondering why changing the length or tension of a string changes its pitch. It all has to do with how fast the string vibrates. If the string vibrates quickly, the pitch is high and if it vibrates slowly, the pitch is low. The next activity will help explain why the speed of vibration affects the pitch.

Extensions

Find an old playing card. (Make sure no one sees you grab it during the card game.) Use a clothespin to attach the card to your bike in such a way that the spokes of the wheel hit the card as you ride along. You may want to ask an adult friend for help since they probably did the same thing to their bike as a kid. Once you have the card attached, ask your friend to ride around you in a circle. Notice that as the spokes go by, they cause the card to vibrate. The faster the wheel moves, the faster the card vibrates. Now get your bike back and ride down the street. Listen carefully as you ride. You'll discover that as you go faster, the card vibrates faster and the pitch gets higher. When you slow down, the pitch gets lower. It's almost like you're riding a musical instrument. Make up a name for your new instrument, *a pitch pedal? . . . a clef cycle? . . . a beat bike?*

The Beat

Materials
- 1 length of string or heavy thread
- 1 metal rod, 10" long (or the longest ½" bolt)
- 1 rubber band guitar
- 1 table knife

Procedure

1. Grab your rubber band guitar. Adjust the tension in two adjoining strings so they produce almost the same note when you pluck them.

2. Pluck the strings together and listen for a "wah, wah" sound that occurs in addition to the sound the strings make by themselves. If you don't hear "wah, wah", adjust the tension slightly in one of the strings and try again. Make sure the notes are about the same pitch. You may also be able to feel a "wah, wah" sound by lightly touching the box. Set your guitar aside and pick up your metal rod.

3. Tie the string or thread onto the middle of the metal rod so that it supports the rod but the rod stays horizontal. Make sure to tie it tightly, so the rod doesn't slip and fall on your toe.

4. Strike the rod with your table knife. Wow, sounds very cool! It sounds much better than before because your fingers no longer interrupt the vibration.

5. Hold the rod by the string or thread, so that it's dangling in front of your face. Don't hold it so close that it smacks you in the nose if it spins a little.

6. Using the table knife, tap the rod so that it spins horizontally. Do you hear an echoing "wah, wah" sound? Although you can probably hear it better with the metal rod, maybe you want to try again with your guitar.

7. Tap the rod again, so that it spins fast and then make it spin slowly. Can you hear a difference in the "wah, wah" sound?

Explanation

Two sounds that are very close in pitch and frequency combine to cause a sound that gets very soft and then very loud. This explains that "wah, wah" sound you heard. The technical name for this effect is **beats**. When the two sounds are extremely close in frequency, the beats are *slow*. When the sounds are further apart in frequency, the beats are *fast*. Musicians tune stringed instruments by playing two different strings that should have the same pitch and listening for beats. When the beats are extremely slow, the two pitches are about the same.

Okay, that helps explain the guitar, but what about the metal rod? Since only the metal rod was vibrating, where did the two pitches that caused the beats come from? It all has something to do with a phenomenon called the **Doppler effect**. When a car or train comes toward you, you hear it making a higher pitched sound than when it's moving away from you. You really notice this effect when a vehicle moves by you and the sound you hear shifts from high to low pitch. Think of what race cars sound like as they whiz by or better yet a fire engine's siren and then you'll have a good idea of the Doppler effect.

The sound is higher when the object comes toward you because the sound waves get bunched up in front of the object. This causes the waves to hit you faster and results in a *higher frequency*. The sound is lower when the object moves away from you because the sound waves are spread out causing a *lower frequency*.

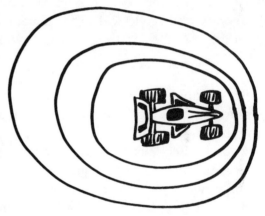

The faster the object moves, the more bunched up in front and spread apart behind, the sound waves get. This makes for a bigger difference between the high pitch coming toward you and the low pitch going away from you.

When you hit the stationary metal rod, it sits still "singing" at one frequency. However, when you spin the rod, part of it's moving toward you and part of it is moving away. As a result of the Doppler effect, the part coming toward you sounds higher than normal and the part moving away sounds lower than normal. You now have two different pitches and these pitches join together to create beats. The faster the rod spins, the greater the difference between the two pitches and the faster the beats. Make sense? Cool . . .

Extensions

Get a friend to try and whistle the same note with you. If one of you changes the frequency you're whistling, you should be able to create beats.

If you go to a rock concert, check out the huge amplifiers on stage. Some of the amplifiers may have something on top that spins around and creates beats in exactly the same way you created beats with your metal rod.

Glob Lobber

Materials

1 test tube   sodium bicarbonate (baking soda)
1 rubber stopper   acetic acid (vinegar)
1 sheet of toilet paper

Procedure

Hold the sheet in your hand and pour about a teaspoon of sodium bicarbonate powder onto the center of the sheet. Fold the sheet in half several times so as to trap the sodium bicarbonate inside a tube-shaped bundle. Set this aside and pull out a test tube. Fill the tube about one-quarter full with acetic acid. Stuff the bundle into the top of the test tube. It may tear slightly, but that's OK. Insert a rubber stopper firmly into the test tube. Hold the tube vertically or it may pop prematurely. All you do to trigger it is to shake, not stir, the test tube up and down mixing the sodium bicarbonate and acetic acid. The rubber stopper will quickly shoot out of the test tube and the stinky glob will lob onto your target.

toilet paper with sodium bicarbonate powder

acetic acid

Explanation

This simple device incorporates the beauty of a chemical reaction with a sudden increase in gas pressure. When sodium bicarbonate and acetic acid combine, they release carbon dioxide gas in huge quantities.

Carbon dioxide is an odorless, colorless gas. The pressure a gas exerts depends on several things: temperature, the size of the container, and the number of gas molecules present. By shaking the test tube up and down, a gigantic increase in the number of carbon dioxide molecules is created in the test tube. These molecules push equally on everything in the test tube while looking for the easiest way out. The stopper moves before anything else and this is where most of the gas "escapes." This causes the stopper to find someplace else to be, and to do so rather quickly. There's enough pressure to push the glob out, too, but only far enough to land in a vinegar-soaked mass on the target.

$$NaHCO_3 \text{ (s)} + CH_3COOH \text{ (ag)} \rightarrow Na^+CH_3COO^- \text{ (aq)} + H_2O \text{ (l)} + CO_2 \text{ (g)}$$

Sodium Bicarbonate   Acetic Acid   Sodium Acetate   Water   Carbon Dioxide

Sticky Fingers

Materials:
 1 clear drinking glass   clear sticky tape
 1 paint brush   talcum powder
 1 piece of black paper

Procedure

1. Grasp the drinking glass firmly, so you leave a nice set of fingerprints. Lightly sprinkle some talc over the area of the glass you just handled.

2. Blow and tap away all excess talc and then, if necessary, gently brush away any remaining globs until you can see a fingerprint or two clearly highlighted. You'll have to practice a bit because this is not a simple task.

3. Once you have a fingerprint outlined, take a strip of tape and press it (sticky side down, please) on top of the "dusted" print. Carefully remove the tape and stick it on the black piece of paper. After some practice, you'll have a fingerprint worth framing (a little secret science agent humor there).

Explanation

Each person has ten unique, unduplicated fingerprints. If you look closely at yours, you see what appears to be lines, loops and circles. They're actually ridges of skin, called **papillae**, that show up very nicely under a magnifying lens. Your skin secretes a material that helps keep it moist and soft. This layer is found everywhere including your fingers. Fingerprints are like rubber stamps and the secretion is like the ink. The ridges get coated, pressed onto a surface and a copy of the curves and whorls is left behind. Depending on the surface type (glass, metal, paper, wood, etc.) and color, various techniques and materials are used to reveal the patterns. It's called "lifting a print" and is a very specialized science. In this case, the talc attaches itself to the oil residue and reveals the print pattern you made on the glass. You can get a pretty good print just by touching your finger to the sticky side of the tape, also. Try other surfaces and colored powders to get the idea. Even though you use very little powder, it does make a mess, so do the clean up, too!

Science Fair Survival Techniques

Go With the Flow

Materials

2 alligator clips   1 length of bell wire, 10"
1 battery, 9-volt   1 nail
1 battery clip, 9-volt   1 paper clip

Procedure

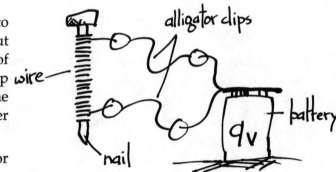

1. Make sure the nail isn't magnetic by trying to pick up the paper clip with it. Remove about one-half inch of the insulation from both ends of the wire. Start with a two-inch tail and wrap the rest of the wire around the nail. Make the wraps tight and close together. Leave another tail at the other end.

2. Snap the clip onto the battery. Use the alligator clip cables to connect the ends of the wire to the battery holder.

3. Use the nail to pick up the paper clip. Try your electromagnet on other objects. Try it without the nail.

Explanation

When an electrical current passes through a loop of copper wire, that loop of wire acts just like a magnet. It will attract objects with iron in them; it has its own magnetic field; and, it will attract or repel other magnets. More loops of wire make a stronger magnet. This is what you created by wrapping the wire around the nail. Finally, the nail strengthens the magnetic field because the nail itself becomes magnetized. The number of loops, the size and number of batteries, and whether or not the wire is insulated influence the properties of your magnet. Try some different arrangements of your materials. A permanent magnet needs no power source. It attracts iron and steel all the time. An electromagnet is a temporary magnet because the flow of electrons can be turned on and off.

This activity and the next one are extensions of the race car activities in the previous section. You might want to do those before tackling these.

Rubber Band 1000

Materials
Your model car from Race III
4 metal washers, 2" diameter
4 fat rubber bands

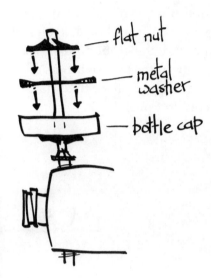

flat nut
metal washer
bottle cap

Procedure

1. Unscrew the two outside flat nuts from the rear axles.

2. Add a metal washer to each side of the rear axle. Screw the flat nuts back onto the axles. Make sure you screw them on in the same direction you did before.

3. Wind up your car the same way you did in Race III (page 27). Set it down, and notice how much better your car performs on the straight-away. Consider the following question: If Newton's second law says that adding mass (washers) to the car makes it harder to change the car's motion, how come the car functions better? Good question, huh? You'll answer it a little later down the road. But you can give it a shot right now if you want.

4. Now take four fat rubber bands and place one each around the outside edge of all four wheels as shown in the illustration. Congratulate your pit crew! These changes just keep making your car run faster and faster. Set your car on the ground and let it go.

5. Ready to do some time trials? Or maybe just tinker under the hood a little while? Try various combinations of washers and rubber bands on both the front and rear wheels. If you have four washers on the front wheels, does it help or hinder your car's movement? Does it help to add washers and/or rubber bands to the front wheels or is it better just to load up the rear wheels? Keep trying different combinations until you get the best possible design for maximum speed. You can get extra washers at any hardware store. Write down your results.

rubber band

Science Fair Survival Techniques

— On Your Own

Explanation

By adding washers and rubber bands, you've improved your car's ability to transfer the **input energy** (a stretched rubber band) to the **motion energy** of your car. It's a fact that you've created a more energy-efficient model car, but something else is going on and it all centers around Newton's Third Law of Motion. Remember that an object, like your car, needs something to push it in order to get moving. Do you ever need a push to get started in the morning? OK, the question in your car's situation is, what does the pushing? It's not the rubber band. What about the wheels? Well, you're partially right. The wheels spin and push against the ground. According to the third law, when the wheels push against the ground, the ground pushes back. So, really the **ground** pushes your car along. No way, you say? Way! Without the extra washers and rubber bands, the wheels didn't make very good contact with the ground. Even though they tried hard to spin, they couldn't push very hard against the ground, so the ground couldn't push back.

The technical term for the force between the wheels and the ground is **friction**. Friction increases between the wheels and the ground the harder they're pushed together. That explains why adding washers to the wheels makes your car run better even though the added mass makes it harder to change the car's motion (Remember that from Newton's second law?). It's important to keep in mind that if you add *too much mass*, the Second Law of Motion takes over and you can forget the race.

Extensions

1. Try replacing the plastic bottle caps with much larger lids. How about four peanut butter jar tops? You'll have to eat a lot of peanut butter sandwiches, but it'll be worth it. You'll see some pretty dramatic results. After you've given this a try, take a look at a 10-speed bike and see if you can figure out why changing to higher gears helps you go faster even though you're actually pedaling slower.

2. One thing that slows down your car is air friction. If you improve the aerodynamics of your car (maybe a nose cone?), you should be able to reduce air friction and increase speed and distance.

3. Let's get off track for a second and think about walking. When you walk, what does the pushing? Hmmm?

Foam Boat 1000

Materials

Your model car from Race II, III, IV
2 foam cylinders
2 foam stars
1 adult pit crew chief
1 big nail
sink or tub with 3-4" of water

Procedure

1. Ask your adult pit crew chief to help you put 3" to 4" of water into a sink or tub. Place your car in the water and notice how well it doesn't float.

2. Rescue your car from the water and dry it off. Remove the outside flat nuts on all four axles. Also remove the metal washers from all four wheels.

3. Screw the inside flat nuts on all four axles until they rest against the slip nuts. Move the plastic wheels until they're up against the flat nuts.

4. Use the big nail and poke a hole in the center of one flat side of both foam cylinders. Take the nail and poke holes through the center of both foam stars.

5. Place the two foam cylinders onto the front axles using the holes you made as a guide. Carefully screw the cylinders into the plastic wheels. Check the pit crew's drawing.

6. Push one star onto each of the rear axles using the holes you made in them as a guide. Make sure you move the stars up against the plastic wheels.

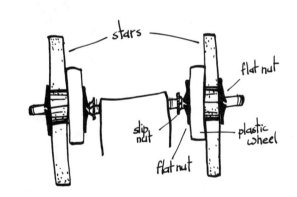

7. With the stars in position, screw one flat nut on the end of both rear axles. Make sure you screw the flat side of the nuts down the axles until they fit snugly against the foam stars.

8. Your car should float now, so let's wind it up and give it a try. Remember to always wind the wheels in the opposite direction you want them to go.

9. With your star paddles in place, you've almost got the Mad Mississippi Gosling. Wind that baby up and let her paddle home.

Science Fair Survival Techniques

Procedure

The first thing you had to consider about your land car was how to make it buoyant so that it would float in water. This was accomplished by using the foam attachments. Next, you had to figure out how to make it move through the water. Remember that in order for the car to get moving, something had to push it. The plastic wheels on your car couldn't push against the water in the same way they push against the ground. The wheels would just slip around because they couldn't get any traction in the water. That's why you made the rear paddle wheels. However, even with paddles, you'll notice that the car doesn't move as smoothly in water as it does on land. There are really two reasons for this poor showing in water. First, a lot of energy is wasted when your car is splashing around. Second, there's much more friction working against your car when you move through water than there is when you move through air.

Extension Ideas

Try to improve the design of your motor boat. Look around the house for things that might make your boat more buoyant. Try adding more foam to the rear of your boat. Maybe you have some packing peanuts around the house you could use. Does this help or hinder how fast your boat moves in water?

Bath Time Balance

Materials

2 paper clips
2 metal washers
1 beaker

1 slotted craft stick
1 length of string

Procedure

1. Bend each of the two paper clips into an "S" shape.

2. Measure the craft stick to find its center. Mark it and tie the string snugly to the craft stick at the mark.

3. Place a bent paper clip in the slots on each end of the stick. You may need to slide the string left or right so that the stick is level and balanced. The wonders of high tech are so cool!

4. Add a washer to each paper clip. If things are out of balance, re-adjust the string again.

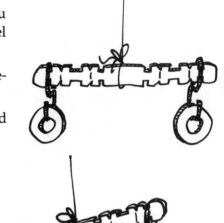

5. Holding the string with one hand, use a finger on the other hard to push up gently on one of the washers. You may want to make a note of what happens even though it seems very simple. Remove your finger and balance the stick again if necessary.

6. Fill the beaker almost full with water.

7. Hold the balance by the string and gently lower one of the washers into the beaker of water. Watch carefully and make a note of what happened. Look familiar?

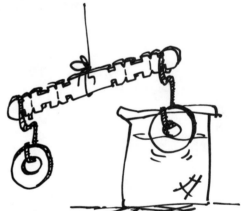

Explanation

Start with the basics. Whenever you push or pull on something, it's being acted on by a force. People can exert forces. So can objects like strings and paper clips. The earth does, too. One of the forces it exerts is called gravity which keeps us on the surface so you can do experiments without floating around. The weight of an object or person is another name for how hard the Earth pulls on it. The little doohicky you just created with the string, craft stick, and paper clips is called a balance. It's used to compare the weight of objects. If the weight of both paper clips is the same, the balance stays level. Gravity is pulling evenly on both objects; both sides weigh the same even though they could be totally different objects. If the weights are different, the balance tips to the heavier side.

Another way to tip the balance is to simply push up on one side (a force), as you did in Step 5. The washer you pushed on didn't weigh any less, you just added an extra upward force (against gravity).

OK. Let's figure out what happened when you dipped one washer in the beaker of water. That side went up. No doubt the washer "all-of-a-sudden" weighed less? Some people like to believe that things weigh less in water — but not you, of course. The water is actually pushing up on the mass, just as your finger did. The force with which water pushes up on things is called a buoyant force.

Science Fair Survival Techniques

Extension Ideas

1. Choose a few waterproof objects from around the house. Weigh them in your hand and get a feel for how heavy they are. Hold them underwater and see what differences in weight you detect. The buoyant force at work!

2. See if you can figure out just how strong the buoyant force is on the washer. Do this by adding paper clips to the stick on the water side and see how many paper clips it takes to make the stick move back to level again.

3. Balance different numbers of washers from different slots on the stick. For example, can you balance two washers on one side with one washer on the other? (Hint: don't use matching slots.) This has nothing to do with bath water, but, hey, it's fun, too! Always remember to ask "What if . . ." when you're experimenting. Some of the best discoveries are made by asking questions.

Bath Time Projectiles

Materials

1 balloon   1 small styrofoam ball
1 cork   1 wash cloth
1 large styrofoam ball

Procedure

1. Blow up the balloon so it's a little bigger than the large styrofoam ball and then tie it off.

2. Use the *Bath-Time Balance* you made in the previous activity and weigh the materials listed above (all except the wash cloth). List them in order from the lightest to the heaviest.

Relative Weight

Lightest object   _____

to   _____

▼   _____

Heaviest object   _____

3. Read this first so you know what to expect, then do it! You're going to hold each object, one at a time, under water on the bottom of a container. Deeper is better. You'll release the object underwater and see how high it "jumps" when it reaches the surface. Before you actually do that, predict which object you think will jump the highest, the lowest, and what the order in between may be.

Predictions

Highest   _____

to   _____

▼   _____

Lowest   _____

4. OK, go for it! Record what actually happens. Remember, you can't force the results.

Actual Results

Highest   _____

to   _____

▼   _____

Lowest   _____

Science Fair Survival Techniques

Explanation

Before doing this activity, lots of people predict that the lighter objects (the cork and the small styrofoam ball) will jump higher than the heavier objects (the balloon and the large Styrofoam ball). If that was your prediction, you were probably thinking about how much easier it is to push around light things than it is to push around heavy things. (That explains why playground bullies never pick on someone their own size.)

While it is true that it's easier to push light objects than heavy objects, there's more than that going on here. When an object is under water, remember there are two forces acting on it: gravity pulling down and the buoyant force of the water pushing up.

If the buoyant force is stronger than gravity, the object may shoot quickly to the surface, like all the things you tested. If gravity is stronger than the buoyant force, the object sinks. If the buoyant force is a lot larger than gravity, the object will appear to "jump up" when it breaks the surface. It's actually still moving because of the push from the buoyant force. So, which object has the largest buoyant force? Yep, the balloon. Which has the next largest buoyant force? The large Styrofoam ball wins this slot. Seems like the size of the object has something to do with it. That's not the whole story, but why give it all away now?

Extension Ideas

1. Trap different amounts of air in the wash cloth and pull it under water. Find the size air bubble necessary for the wash cloth to rise to the surface when you let go.

2. Get several balloons and blow them up to different sizes. Which ones jump farthest from the surface when you release them from the bottom of the tub? Try writing a law that will explain your results then test it.

Sinkable Styrofoam

Materials

6 metal washers	cooking oil
2 paper clips	hard-boiled egg
1 beaker	salt
1 large Styrofoam ball	water
1 small Styrofoam ball	

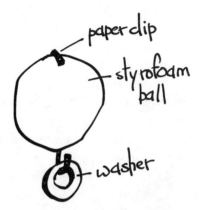

Procedure

1. Do your best to straighten two paper clips (don't use the ones from your balance). Bend a hook on one end of each of them so they look like a skinny "J".

2. Push a paper clip through each Styrofoam ball so that the hook end is close to the ball's surface. Bend the opposite end to keep the clip in place. You should end up with something like the drawing. Make sure they float. Hang a washer on each hook and check that each ball still floats.

4. Predict which ball will hold the most washers before it sinks and how many washers it'll take to sink it. Test your prediction.

5. Now comes some precision measuring. Fill the beaker with water to the 70 ml mark.

6. Place the large Styrofoam ball and hook (no washers) in the beaker so it floats. Look at the water level on the side of the beaker. It should be about 75 ml. This means that the Styrofoam ball displaces 5 ml of water: (75 ml - 70 ml = 5 ml). Your measurements may differ slightly but you get the idea.

7. Hook one washer to the large Styrofoam ball. You may have to push the hook of the clip into the ball so the washer is pulled against the ball and can't hang down and touch the container.

8. Place the Styrofoam ball and washer in the beaker of water. Record how much water it displaces. Repeat for two and three washers.

Water Displaced

	Large	*Small*
Ball alone	5 ml	
Ball plus 1 washer		
Ball plus 2 washers		
Ball plus 3 washers		

9. Repeat steps 5-8 for the small Styrofoam ball.

On Your Own

Explanation

If you've been paying attention, you already know that there are two forces acting on something that's in water: gravity and a buoyant force. When something is floating, these two forces are equal. In other words, they cancel each other out and the object floats merrily along.

Adding a washer to the Styrofoam ball increases the force of gravity. If the ball is going to float, then the buoyant force must get larger, too.

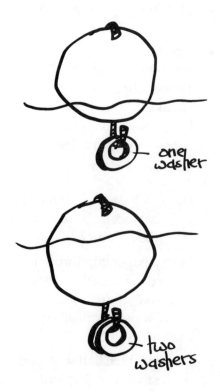

one washer

How does the buoyant force get larger? The object has to displace more water. Watch closely and you'll see the ball sink lower in the water as you add washers. It turns out that the buoyant force depends entirely on how much water an object displaces. More water displaced gives you a larger buoyant force. In fact, *the buoyant force is equal to the weight of the water that's displaced by the object.* Too cool!

two washers

This little fact is known as **Archimedes' Principle**, and was discovered by none other than that great bathtub scientist Archimedes. Legend has it that Archimedes figured all this out while he was in an overflowing tub. He had suddenly solved a big problem with this fact and was so excited he jumped out of the bath, ran into the street, and yelled "Eureka!" which means, "I've found it!" Hopefully, he held a towel over himself.

So, if you somehow double the weight of an object, it must displace twice as much water in order to float because it now needs twice the buoyant force. The small ball and the large ball should displace about the same amount of water with one washer attached because they require the same buoyant force to hold up one washer. Finally, the large Styrofoam ball can hold more washers before sinking because it displaces more water due to its larger size. Makes sense.

Eureka!!

Extensions

1. See if the water level in the beaker (try 70 ml) has any effect on how much water a Styrofoam ball displaces.

2. Blow up a balloon to exactly the size of the large Styrofoam ball. See how many washers it takes to sink the balloon compared to how many it takes to sink the Styrofoam ball. You may be surprised.

3. A certain amount of cooking oil weighs less than the same amount of water because it's less dense. If the buoyant force depends on the weight of the fluid that's displaced, cooking oil should give you different results than water. Repeat some of the experiments in this activity substituting cooking oil for water. Find out how your results may change.

4. A way to alter how much water weighs is to add salt to it. That changes the buoyant force. Use different amounts of salt in water to test this idea. You can also use it for a magic trick. A hard boiled egg will sink in plain water, but if you add enough salt to the water, the egg will float. Ah, the wonders of science!

On Your Own

Clay Boats and Ocean Liners

Materials
1 stick of clay
sink or tub of water

Procedure
1. Fill a sink or tub with water. Ask an adult if you need help. Just for science, drop the clay into some water. If it doesn't sink, you've got some strange clay or there may be aliens in your water. When the clay sinks, which force is greater: the force of gravity pulling down or the buoyant force of the water pushing up?

3. Rescue the clay and figure out what you can do to make it float. It might take a moment to get it right, so be patient. Hint: something that looks like a boat might work!

Explanation
When the clay is in a big lump, it sinks. That means the force of gravity pulling down, is greater than the buoyant force pushing up. Buoyant force depends on how much water something pushes out of the way. That's called **displacement**. When it was just a lump, you could say that the clay didn't displace enough water to counteract gravity. The trick is to shape the clay so it displaces more water, thus increasing the buoyant force under it. If you flatten the clay into a thin sheet and fold up the sides, it'll displace lots more water and float. Gravity hasn't changed; the buoyant force has increased. That's how it's possible to float a huge ship made of steel.

Extension Ideas
1. Have a contest with friends to see whose clay boat can hold the largest number of washers, marbles, rocks, etc., before sinking.

2. Try this activity with aluminum foil. What changes do you expect to make? How much of the winning load from #1 can it hold before sinking?

Clay Heads and Keels

Materials
2 craft sticks
2 metal washers

1 stick of clay
sink or tub of water

Procedure

1. Break off a small chunk (about one-eighth) of the clay and set it aside.

2. Take the remaining clay and shape it into a long, narrow vessel that looks something like a canoe.

3. Fill a sink or tub with water. Make sure your boat floats by putting a couple of metal washers inside it on the bottom. With the boat on the water, use a finger to tap the sides called gunwales (gún-als) and watch it rock back and forth. See how close you can get it to the water before it rolls over (capsizes) and sinks. Note how hard you had to push it.

4. If everything's ship shape, take the boat out of the water. Pick up the clay you set aside. Use a little to hold the two sticks together and pretend this is a person.

5. Use some clay on one end of the "person" and stand them up in the middle of the boat. Make sure you don't push the sticks all the way through the bottom of the boat. It's only clay! Use any remaining clay to put a large head on the sticks.

6. With your "person" added, set the boat on the water and see how well it floats. The rule is: only a clay head would stand up in a small boat. Tip your boat the same way you did for #3 and notice any changes.

7. Rescue your boat and the clay head and make him "lie down" in the boat. Test it the same way (by tipping) and see what changes there may be.

8. Use a little clay to attach the two metal washers to the outside bottom of your boat so that they're flat against it. Try the same two tipping activities as #3 and #6. Notice anything different?

9. This may be a little tricky so get some help if you want it. Remove the washers and turn them so that they point straight down from the outside bottom of the boat and are in line with the length of the boat. Repeat Steps #3 and #6 and make a note of differences.

On Your Own

Explanation

So, what is it that makes a small boat tip over more easily when some clay head stands up in it? It can't be the extra weight or the boat would have sunk when you added washers in #3 or tried #7. To understand what's going on, you first need to know something about the center of gravity. An object's center of gravity is sort of the average position of all the stuff in it. For example, the center of gravity of a ball is at its center. The center of gravity of a craft stick is in the middle. The center of gravity is where the force of gravity acts on something.

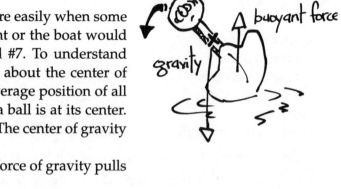

Here's an end view of a boat that's floating. The force of gravity pulls down, and buoyant force pushes up.

Now, suppose the boat tips a little bit. Gravity still pulls on the center of gravity of the boat, but the buoyant force shifts over because a different part of the boat is now displacing the water. Check out the diagram and notice that the two forces combine to rotate the boat back to an upright position.

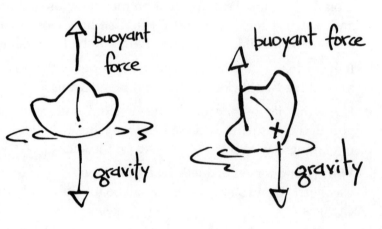

Look at what happens when you add a clay-headed person to the boat. When the person is lying down, the center of gravity of "boat + person" is pretty much in the same place it was before you added the person: low down in the boat. If the person is standing up, though, the center of gravity shifts with them and is now much higher.

Now tip the boat and because the center of gravity is so high, the combination of the upward buoyant force and the downward force of gravity acts to roll the boat right on over instead of back up safely. It's easy to prevent this problem: Tell the clay head to sit down! There are other ways, too. Add weight to the bottom (like the washers) of the boat so the center of gravity stays low even if some twit stands up. This is called ballast. Some boats have a keel on the bottom that makes the boat very stable and less likely to roll over. That's what you made in #9.

Extension Ideas

1. Figure out why freighters carry oil and other cargo down inside the boat instead of on the deck.

2. Grab hold of one of those drinking cups for toddlers that don't fall over even when they tip. Figure out how it works.

3. What happens if you add more washers to the bottom of the boat as in #8?

4. Bigger washers might make more of a difference for #9. You could try pushing a small putty knife through the clay from the inside and see what kind of a keel it would make. Be sure to seal the clay around the blade. Duh.

Long Range Water

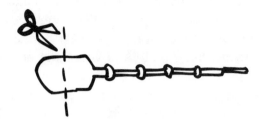

Materials

    1 pipette
    1 rubber stopper, 1-hole
    1 two-liter bottle
        scissors
        water

Procedure

1. Do this one outside or at least in a sink or tub! Fill the two-liter bottle with water and give it a big squeeze. Not such a great squirt bottle, is it? The water gooshes nicely, but it doesn't really squirt.

2. Fill the bottle again and twist the 1-hole stopper firmly into the opening. Squeeze the bottle again, but be careful where you aim this time. Getting better. Be thinking about why this is happening.

3. This part is a little tricky, so read the directions and look at the pictures carefully. Cut off the bulb end of the pipette as shown and then put it pointing backwards through the 1-hole stopper. Some cooking oil or soap may help if it's a tight fit.

4. Fill the bottle again and put the stopper firmly in place. Squeeze again, and really be careful where you aim.

Explanation

Have you figured it out, yet? To make a better (further shooting and faster moving) squirt bottle, you forced the water to go through smaller and smaller openings. Here's why it happened.

Think about a liquid moving through a pipe. The pipe begins with a large diameter and gradually narrows to a small diameter.

As a smaller volume of the water starts to pass through the narrowing pipe, it must speed up because of the push from the larger volume of water behind it. This is similar to what a river does when it encounters a narrower channel. A low velocity in the larger section changes to a high velocity in the smaller section. The two-liter bottle is a simple application of this principle. You squeeze the large-diameter bottle and push the water at a low speed. The low-velocity water is forced through a small opening at the top. That means it has to exit at a much higher velocity to stay ahead of the huge volume of water pushing it.

If you want to be exact about things (and that's OK sometimes), there is a formula that describes precisely how the velocity changes. It is:

$$A_1 v_1 = A_2 v_2$$

or, in other words:

(cross-sectional area at one diameter) x (velocity at that diameter) =

        (cross-sectional area at second diameter) x (velocity at that diameter)

Gravity also figures into the question: How far will it squirt? Without gravity, the water would just cruise merrily along in a straight line until it hit something. With gravity, the water changes directions. If you shoot straight up, the water goes up and then comes back down. Your distance is zero and you get wet. If you shoot the water horizontally, the downward pull of gravity gradually causes it to bend toward the ground and you shoot only a short way. Obviously, it would be better to shoot the water somewhere in between straight up and level. This is ideal because the water can reach its best horizontal distance given its velocity even though gravity continuously pulls down. The best angle for maximum distance is halfway between up and horizontal, or about 45°.

So, the velocity, you give it by squeezing a certain amount, and the angle you give it by pointing it a certain direction, will determine who gets a soaking from your squirt bottle. Oh, be sure you can run faster than they can, too.

Extension Ideas

1. Grab a squirt gun and explain how it works in terms of forcing water to go from a large diameter to a small diameter opening.

2. Feeling mathematical? Using the formula for the area of a circle (πr^2), show that by making water go through an opening one-tenth the diameter of your two-liter bottle, you increase its speed 100 times. Such fun!

3. You might also want to calculate the velocity of the water moving in the two-liter pop bottle. To do this, measure the cross-sectional area of both the pipette opening and the bottle, then measure a specific distance from the squirt bottle to a target — say twenty feet. Have a friend with a stop watch time how long it takes for the water to travel the twenty feet. Using these values, figure out the velocity of the water in the bottle using the equation $A_1 v_1 = A_2 v_2$. By the way, this is a tough challenge. Better know a little physics or talk to someone who does before you tackle it.

Tense Water

Materials
  2 corks
  1 beaker
  1 pipette
    liquid soap
    pepper
    water

Procedure

1. Fill the beaker as full as possible with water. Set it on a flat surface. By the way, make sure the surface is level, smooth, and hard. Look for a place where it won't matter when (not _if_) you spill the water and make a mess. Counter tops near a sink are OK, tables must be protected, and outside may be best. Working in a sink is ideal but it's hard to see the results sometimes.

2. Fill the pipette with water (not from the beaker) and begin adding shots of water to the beaker. This is best done while viewing the beaker at eye level. You may have to bend down a little bit to look straight across the surface of the water.

3. Add drops of water until the water bulges higher than the beaker and finally overflows. Eyes at water-level provide the best oooh-aaah viewing.

4. Empty the beaker and fill it again almost to the top . . . uh, with water.

5. Sprinkle some pepper over the surface of the water. Watch how the pepper reacts on the water.

6. Take your pipette and dip it into your liquid soap. Now touch the center of the water's surface with the pipette. What happens? Pepper doesn't like soap. Just kidding! It's much more interesting than that! Pour out the water and rinse the beaker.

7. Now, float the two corks on some water. Nudge them very close to each other, but don't let them touch.

8. Let go of the corks. They must know each other. Actually, the water is in charge here.

Science Fair Survival Techniques

Explanation

All three of the things you observed have to do with something called surface tension. Water almost seems to have a "skin" on it. One way of explaining surface tension is to see how those iddy-biddy things called water molecules behave. Water molecules are polar molecules, which means one side of the molecule is positive and the other is negative. Because positives and negatives attract each other, all the water molecules in a beaker or bathtub or ocean tend to hang onto one another. It's sort of a big ol' group hug. They "hug" each other so hard that some molecules can hang over the sides of a beaker. The ones on the inside won't let their buddies fall off of the edge until there's just too many of them and gravity wins the tug-o-war.

Soap molecules are huge compared to water molecules and they're grouped together in long chains. One end of the chain is attracted to water and the rest of the chain isn't. A soap molecule grabs a water molecule and breaks up the group hug. The soap and water molecules form a thin film of their own. In other words, the soap breaks the surface tension of the water by "disconnecting" the water molecules from each other.

Suppose you have some pepper "catching rays" and floating on the surface tension provided by the water molecules. Some gigantic soap molecules show up and hook onto the nearest water molecule. This breaks the surface tension and creates a film that spreads out from where the soap touched the water. The water molecules that were in that spot are pulled away by the attraction of their unaffected buddies. This yanks water molecules to the side and the pepper goes along for the ride.

What about those corks? Do they really like each other? Nah, it's the water molecules grabbing on to each other again. When the corks get close to each other, the water molecules in between have a choice. They can either be attracted to the cork or to all the rest of their water buddies. It turns out that cork is a non-polar molecule (there are no positive and negative ends). Water doesn't like non-polar molecules so it zips to its buddies and allows the corks to come together in the process.

Extensions

1. If you carefully lay a pin on the surface of an almost overflowing cup of water, it will "float" on the surface tension of the water. Lay the pin on a small piece of tissue paper and set the tissue on the water. Use a toothpick to gently poke the tissue down and away from the pin. The surface tension of the water will hold the pin up. Try it and then see what happens when you add a little soap to the water holding the pin.

2. See how many drops of water you can get on a penny. Then rub the penny with soap and have your friend try it. Good luck!

3. Read up on water striders and other critters that use surface tension to get around on a pond or stream.

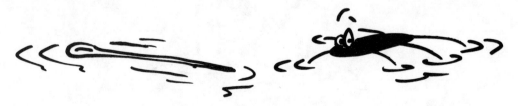

Rubber Bands and Steel Girders

This activity has to be about muscles and bones. (It is.)

Materials

    3 paper tubes
    2 elastic cords
    2 ping-pong balls
    2 pipe cleaners
    1 body (probably yours)
    1 craft stick
    1 egg shell or chicken bone
    1 red crayon
      acetic acid (vinegar)

Procedure

1. Start with yourself. With your writing hand, palpate (touch carefully), the hard places (bones) and the soft stuff (muscles) under the skin in your other arm from your elbow to your fingers. Figure out, just from touching, how many bones you have in your lower arm, wrist, and hand. Try the same thing for a leg from your knee to your toes. No cheating — don't look at any skeleton diagrams!

2. Now, look carefully at a joint (where two bones come together) such as your elbow, knee, wrist, shoulder, and knuckles. Not all joints move and these are harder to find. Moveable joints are very different. Feel along the back of your knees, in your arm pits, and the top side of your elbows. You'll find stringy, cord-like things near these joints.

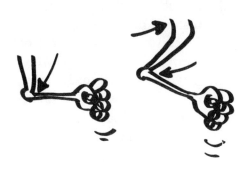

3. Study the "range of motion" of your joints. For example, your elbow joint bends only one way, but not the other. However, your shoulder joint allows you to move your arm in a complete circle. What movement do you have with your knee? Put your findings into categories:

Move in one direction only _____

_____

Move in almost a complete circle _____

_____

Hard to move by themselves (other joints move, too) _____

_____

— On Your Own —

Explanation

1. Grab two of the paper tubes. These will represent bones to be joined together. In this case, the joint could be your knee, knuckle, wrist, or elbow. In some cases, one tube may represent more than one bone. For example, you probably discovered that your lower arm and lower leg contain two bones each, called the **radius** and **ulna** [úl-nah] in your arm and the **tibia** [tíh-bee-ah] and **fibula** [fíh-bu-lah] in your leg. OK, now you can look at a skeleton picture.

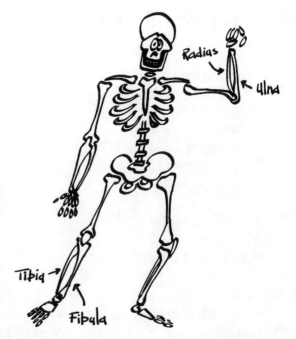

2. Punch four small holes in one end of each tube about ¾ inch from the opening. The holes should be evenly spaced around the tube, as shown. Make sure they're big enough for the elastic cord to slide through.

3. Slip one end of the elastic cord through opposite holes in one tube and continue through opposite holes in the second tube. Tie the cord loosely so you can hold the tubes apart about an inch without stretching the cord.

4. Place a ping-pong ball between the tubes, as shown. The fit should be snug and the cord slightly stretched but you should be able to move the "bones" freely around the ball. Congratulations! You've just joined your bones with muscles, tendons, and cartilage. The ping-pong ball represents **cartilage** (a material that supports and cushions bones). Before birth, bones are actually all cartilage. As you get older, the cartilage in the middle of the bone hardens and stops growing. The ends stay "soft" and add bone cells making the bone longer and you taller! This is the **epiphysis** (ih-píf-eh-ses] the end of a long bone where most growth occurs). The elastic cord represents both muscles and **tendons** (the stringy things that connect muscles to bones or cartilage).

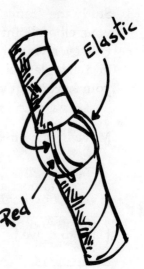

5. To improve your model a bit, take a red crayon and color the middle sections of the elastic cord. The red part of the cords are muscle and the white parts are tendons (sort of close to the actual colors even). Muscles expand and contract, causing bones to move. To see how this happens, gather the "muscle" together on one side of the bones. This should cause the joint to bend toward the shorter muscle.

Notice that the muscle on the other side of the bones stretches in the opposite direction. Muscles in your body work in pairs like this. Those on one side of a joint get smaller while the ones on the other side get longer. To bend the bones the other way, the muscles that were stretching must contract and the ones that were contracting, must now stretch.

6. Your joint is probably pretty loose and can easily move all over the place. This is like your shoulder or hip, which are called "ball and socket" joints. Other joints are more restricted in their movement. To strengthen your joint and restrict its movement, thread a pipe cleaner through the remaining holes in the tubes. This is easier if you remove the cartilage (ping-pong ball) before using the pipe cleaner. It's not brain surgery but it still takes some patience. Be sure to replace the "cartilage" and then twist the pipe cleaner until the joint is snug.

The pipe cleaner represents **ligaments** (dense, tough tissue that connects bones to bones). The ligaments you added restrict the range of motion of the cardboard tubes so they operate more like a knee or elbow joint. Of course, you can't bend your knee or elbow both ways, like your model. Hmmm, if you can do this, see what the circus will pay you and forget school . . . just kidding.

7. To further restrict the movement of your joint, tape the craft stick to your model as shown. This makes it so your joint can bend in one direction only.

In your knee joint, the craft stick represents your **patella** (knee cap). In your elbow, this restraint is caused by a piece of the **humerus** ([húe-mer-us] upper arm) that overlaps the **radius** and **ulna** (the bones of the lower arm). Joints occur any place bones come together. As mentioned earlier, not all joints in your body are like the one you just built. Some joints don't move at all. For example, the bones of your skull start out separate and then grow and fuse together as you get older. When you're born, you have about 275 bones. By the time you're fully grown, that number is down to 206 because many bones fuse together at a joint and, in effect, become one bone.

Extension Ideas

1. To demonstrate that bones are made primarily of calcium, soak a chicken bone in acetic acid which is white vinegar. The vinegar removes the calcium (see the very scientific equation below) and leaves the bone a mushy, rubbery mass . . . cool. The bone is primarily made of hydroxyapatite, but it also has calcium carbonate — just like egg shells. The egg shells will turn to goo much faster than the bone because they have more calcium carbonate.

$$CaCO_3 \text{ (s)} + 2CH_3COOH \text{ (aq)} \longrightarrow Ca^{+2}(CH3COO^-)_2 \text{ (aq)} + H_2O \text{ (l)} + CO_2 \text{ (g)}$$

| Calcium Carbonate | Acetic Acid | Calcium Acetate | Water | Carbon Dioxide |

It takes a few days, so you may want to start some eggs soaking now. Do two or three in separate containers of white vinegar. Make sure there aren't any cracks in the shell before you soak them. Leave them in the vinegar so they'll pickle and toughen the membrane for the activity.

2. Try adding another joint to the one you've already made. Now you're close to what a finger looks like.

3. Why does it hurt when you sprain an ankle?

4. Find out the differences between voluntary and involuntary muscles. Which are more important?

5. Some football players have had their knees so banged up that they have their anterior cruciate ligament (You're on your own on this one) removed. So, you <u>can</u> play football without this ligament. What happens if you have a major tendon removed?

An Eye For Your Eye

Light + chemistry + neurons = "Oh, I see!"

Materials

    1 animal eye (sheep, cow, pig, and so on…[keep it in the fridge])
    1 candle
    1 pair of latex gloves
    1 plastic lens, 1" diameter
    1 pie tin
    1 sharp knife or good quality scissors
    1 white balloon
      matches
      an adult to help

Procedure

1. Start by wearing the gloves and having adult help. It's OK to handle the eye without gloves if it's sealed in the bag. If you open the bag, wear the gloves. This is a preserved specimen but gloves are always a smart idea.

2. Open the bag containing the eye and place the eye in the pie tin. Pick it up and look at the outside structures. Describe what you see and what it feels like. Locate the hard "stem" coming out of the back of the eye. It may be covered slightly and hard to find but it is very different from any other feature on the eyeball.

3. The tan colored material surrounding the eyeball is muscle tissue. If you look closely, you'll see little "lines" in it. These are the muscles that help move, turn, and hold the eye in its socket. There is also some light colored fatty material and perhaps some skin tissue attached as well. You may be able to see the white eyeball itself under this material. The dark circle is the front of the eye and the hard stem is the back of the eye. It's truly amazing!

4. The best thing to do is trim almost all of the material off of the eyeball except the stem. Under adult supervision, use a sharp knife, razor knife, or dissecting scissors to do this. The eyeball is tough but be careful. Oh, and watch out for your soft fingers inside your soft gloves, too! When you're finished, you'll have a sphere with a stubby tail . . . or . . . something like that. Disposal is easy: the material you've cut off can be wrapped in plastic and safely tossed in the garbage.

5. This step is a little difficult. Look at the drawing and get an idea of what you're going to do. The best way to start is to poke a small hole and then cut all the way around with sharp scissors as shown on the next page. Get some help if you need it! When you're done, the eye may separate into two halves — one with the hard stem (back of the eye) and the other with the dark circle (front of the eye). You may need to actually cut the clear, jelly-like goo and the floppy, gray tissue inside the eye if the halves don't separate easily. Be careful and take your time!

6. You're finished cutting so pause and explore a little. Be careful not to rip or tear. Respect for all forms of life applies here! This is truly a remarkable device you're studying. Take your time and really look closely at the two halves in the dish. They're very different from each other. Find all the things labeled in the diagram.

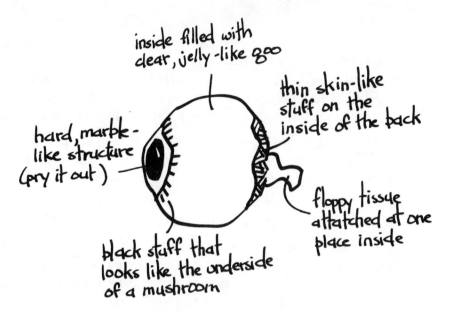

inside filled with clear, jelly-like goo

thin skin-like stuff on the inside of the back

hard, marble-like structure (pry it out)

floppy tissue attached at one place inside

black stuff that looks like the underside of a mushroom

Wondering what all this stuff does? Curious about what to call it? You'll find out as you continue.

7. Place the specimen in the pie tin, cover it with plastic, and set it aside so you can refer to it later. Be sure to gather all the pieces when you're finished and dispose of them within one day. Take off your gloves by pulling from the wrist to the fingers, turning them inside out. Toss them in the garbage.

Extensions

1. Below you'll see a "dot" on the left and an "X" on the right. Hold this book straight in front of you and close to your eyes. Close your left eye and stare at the dot with your right eye.

2. While staring at the dot, slowly move the book away from your face. Keep staring at the dot with your right eye. At a certain distance, the "X" will completely disappear.

3. Now, repeat it, but this time, close your right eye and stare at the "X" with your left eye. Hold the book the same way and move it slowly away from you. At some point the dot will disappear. What happens if you keep moving the book slowly away from your eyes?

Explanation

NOTE: To explain what you saw in the specimen and what you observed with your own eye, you're going to build a model with a balloon and a plastic lens. It's not exact, by any means, but it'll help you get a better idea of how your eye works. You'll need an adult for some of this too, so see if there's one available.

1. Hold the plastic lens over these words, move it back and forth, and see what it does to them. Yep, it's a magnifying lens. Actually, it's used to bend light. Notice that it has the same general shape as the hard, marble-like thing you found in the specimen eye. The purpose of a lens in an eyeball is to bend light to a point on the back of the eye. The lens in your specimen was probably cloudy, but that's just from the preservative. It's normally clear so light can pass through it easily.

2. Blow up the balloon to about volleyball size and slip the plastic lens inside the neck of the balloon. Some air may escape, but that's OK. Try to keep most of it in the balloon. This might be easier with some help from a friend. Turn the lens sideways so it seals the neck of the balloon.

3. Move the lens as far forward as possible in the neck so there's a large opening for light to go through to the inside of the balloon.

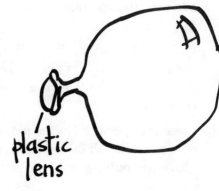

4. The white balloon represents the **sclera** ([ss-cléar-ah] the white part of your eye). The neck of the balloon that's holding the lens represents your **iris** ([í-rus] the colored part of your eye). You could color it to match your own eyes. Inside a real eye is a jelly-like goo called vitreous humor [víh-tree-us]. The vitreous humor helps the eye keep its shape and cushions it against injury. It's supposed to be crystal clear so you can't see it unless you open the eye. Uh, don't do that to your eye; that's why you have the specimen.

plastic lens

5. If you look into the lens, the opening in the center that goes to the back of the eye is the **pupil** (the black center of a real eye). Pinch the lens on its edge through the balloon and give the balloon a slow, circular twist. If you twist it enough, the neck of the balloon will close off and not let in any light. This is what the iris does to protect the eye from really bright light. The muscles that look like the black underside of a mushroom are called **ciliary muscles** (sílly-airy). They surround the pupil on the inside your specimen. Open and close the iris to let in more or less light. You saw this happen if you did the mirror and flashlight thing. A real pupil can't close all the way, like your model, and a real pupil is in front of the lens, not behind it like your model.

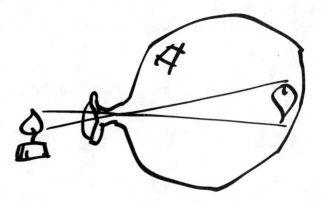

6. Practice this before you light the candle. Hold the balloon so the lens is about four inches from the candle. It's easier if you lay your arms on the table so you can keep the balloon steady. Check the diagram.

7. Get the room as dark as you can and light the candle. LAB SAFETY: An adult **must** help you when you use a candle!

8. Slowly move the balloon towards or away from the candle until you see a clear, sharp image of the flame at the center of the back of the balloon. Notice that the image is upside down. This is what happens in real eyes. Your brain analyzes the image and turns it right side up.

The back of the balloon eye is like the **retina** ([réh-tin-ah] the gray, floppy tissue inside the back half of your specimen) in a real eye. The retina absorbs incoming light and chemically changes it to electrical impulses that travel along nerve cells to the brain for analysis. The retina contains a black pigment layer (which gives the pupil its black color), rod cells for seeing black and white, and cone cells for seeing color.

9. The retinal nerve cells clump together into that little hard stem on the outside back of the eyeball. It's called the optic nerve. By the way, there are no light receptors where the retina attaches to the optic nerve. When light hits that part inside your eye, there's nothing to receive it. Voilá! This is your blind spot or optic disk which you found with the "dot and the X" activity.

10. Turn the balloon slowly left and right and watch the image of the flame. It moves in the opposite direction. This means that things to the right of us form an image on the left side of the retina, and vice versa. It's amazing how your brain figures out all this stuff!

Extension Ideas

1. Sometimes as you stare off into the sky (never at the sun!), the ceiling, or a white wall, you'll see a speck fall slowly across your field of vision. It seems to move when you blink and then start flowing with gravity again. These "floaters" are actually microscopic particles in the vitreous humor inside your eye!

2. Here's how to model nearsightedness and farsightedness with your balloon eye. This will help explain why some people need glasses.

   a) Get and keep a sharp image of the candle flame. Same safety rules apply!

   b) Squeeze the balloon together top to bottom so that it gets slightly longer. Try to keep the lens the same distance from the flame as you do this. The image of the flame is now blurry because the focal point is in front of the retina inside the eye. If you can hold this shape and move the "eye" closer to the candle, the image will sharpen slightly. This is nearsightedness. Glasses are used to bend the light outward before it enters the eye, so that after it passes through the eye's lens, it's focused on the retina and a clear image is produced. That's hard to do with the simple model you have, but many of us are glad it works for real!

   c) Repeat (a) except this time, squeeze the balloon front to back so that it gets slightly shorter. Keep that lens the same distance from the flame. Again, the image is blurry but, this time, it's because the focal point is behind the retina outside the eye. Hold and move the squeezed "eye" away from the flame to get a clearer image. You've modeled farsightedness. To correct this vision, glasses would be used to bend the light inward before it enters the eye. That way, the eye's lens will have a better chance to bend it to a focus on the retina.

3. Ask an eye doctor how it's possible to "see" the blood flowing in your retina.

__ On Your Own __

Take a Breather

Materials
2 pipettes
2 small balloons
1 bottle, two-liter
1 candle
1 clear jar or glass
1 handy adult
1 large, clear balloon
1 length of plastic tubing
1 mirror
   rubber bands
   scissors
   tape (any kind)

Procedure

1. Breathe in; breathe out! You didn't need to be told how to do that one, huh? Notice what your body does as you breathe. What moves? What do you feel?

2. Have that adult of choice help you and light the candle. Put it on a table.

3. Place the jar over the candle (carefully, so you don't blow it out) as shown. Count or use a second hand on a clock to determine how long it takes the candle to go out. This is your comparison time.

4. Repeat Step 3. However, breathe into the jar before you place it over the candle. Time this one, too.

5. Do it again. This time, hold your breath for 10 seconds and then breathe into the jar. Time the candle.

6. Repeat; hold your breath for 20 seconds; 30 seconds; 5 minutes (just checking your alertness level).

7. Exhale (breathe out) on the mirror. What do you see on the mirror?

Explanation

You probably already know that your lungs get oxygen into your body. Equally as important is that they get rid of carbon dioxide, which is a waste product. The candle in the jar showed you that. A candle needs oxygen to burn. Carbon dioxide puts out a flame. The more carbon dioxide there is, the quicker the candle is put out. It took a shorter and shorter time for the candle to go out as you held your breath longer. That's because holding your breath causes the quantity of carbon dioxide to be exhaled from your lungs to increase. Besides bringing in oxygen and getting rid of carbon dioxide, the lungs also get rid of water from your body. That's what that stuff on the mirror was: water vapor condensed into droplets.

So, how do these lungs work? Build this model and it should show you.

1. Grab both of your pipettes and a pair of scissors. Find an adult to help you cut the pipettes in two places as shown in the illustration to the right.

2. Slip the two pipette bulbs together, so it looks like the next picture. You can hold them together with tape if you want, then cut off the tops of the bulbs as shown. What you will end up with is a "Y" connector.

3. Insert your new "Y"-shaped piece into the tubing and tape it in place. Attach the two small balloons to the arms of the "Y" with rubber bands.

4. Grab the two-liter bottle and soak it in hot water so you can easily get the base off of the bottle.

5. Using a sharp knife or scissors (Did someone mention having an adult around?), cut off the very bottom of the bottle, leaving a little bit of the bottom curve for support.

6. Insert the tubing through the bottom of the bottle and out through the neck. Use tape and seal the tubing at the neck so the balloons are suspended inside the bottomless bottle.

7. Cut the neck off the large, clear balloon. Stretch the rest of the balloon over the bottom of the bottle. If necessary, use a rubber band to keep it in place. It needs to be in place snugly and slightly stretched.

8. Pull on the bottom balloon, as shown. Watch what happens to the small balloons.

What does this all mean, you ask? Read on.

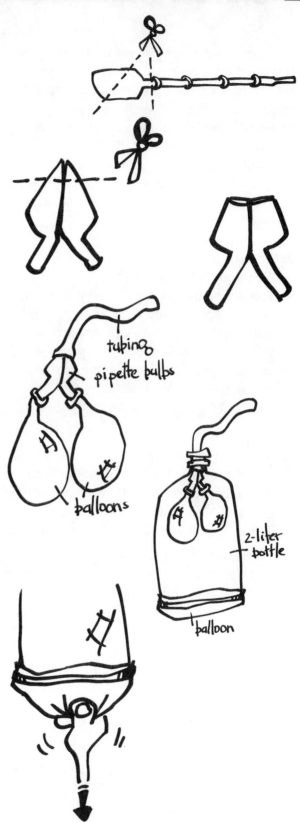

tubing
pipette bulbs
balloons

2-liter bottle
balloon

© 1997 Rev 1999 The Wild Goose Co.

Science Fair Survival Techniques

The long tube at the top represents your **trachea** ([tráy-key-uh] where the air comes in). The two arms of the plastic piece represent **bronchial tubes** ([brón-key-ul] lead to the lungs). The small balloons are the lungs. The bottom balloon represents the **diaphragm** (díe-uh-fram) a large muscle under the lungs. When you pull on it, you lower the pressure inside the bottle (your chest cavity). This causes the balloons/lungs to inflate because the outside air pressure is now higher than the inside air pressure and air rushes in to equalize it. When you let go of the diaphragm, you increase the inside air pressure and the lungs deflate as the air rushes out. The diaphragm (with help from other muscles) pulls air into the lungs and then pushes it out again. While the air is inside, the lungs collect carbon dioxide out of and put oxygen back into your blood. The carbon dioxide is then shoved out with the next exhale. It's a great system!

Extension Ideas

1. Put your finger over the "trachea" or slightly pinch the tube of your model. This represents something blocking the airway, like a big piece of food that was swallowed too quickly. Pull on the diaphragm and see what, if anything, happens. Now, push hard on the diaphragm and see what happens. This controlled, upward thrust of the diaphragm is just what you do with the **Heimlich Maneuver** ([híme-lick]). You push hard on the diaphragm and force extra air out of the lungs. This push of air is usually enough to dislodge whatever is stuck in the airway and allow regular breathing to resume.

2. There are some fascinating things you can discover about ordinary sneezes and coughs and why your respiratory system needs them. See what the library has to offer on these subjects.

3. Asthma is a lifelong condition that afflicts many people and can be brought on by stress, allergies, or other illnesses. People without asthma are clueless about what it's like to gasp for every breath and not find your inhaler. If you have asthma, you understand. If not, try running in place for several minutes. Then, when you're breathing heavily, pinch your nose and breathe only through a straw. Remember, when you panic and yank out the straw to get more air, asthmatics can't do that.

4. Check with a respiratory specialist at a hospital to find out how to measure your lung capacity. They can show you some amazing things about those two balloons inside you and help you understand treatments for lung illnesses.

Sun Time

Materials
- 1 handy clock
- 1 paper clip
- 1 pen or marker
- 1 piece of poster board, 3' x 3'
- 1 plastic triangular wedge
- 1 protractor
- 1 ruler
- 1 sheet of paper
- 1 stick of clay
- 1 string
- 1 sun (already in the sky)
- 1 wooden dowel

Procedure I

1. The first thing you need to do is find out which direction is **geographic north** (the direction of the north geographic pole, not magnetic north like a compass indicates). To find geographic north, all you need is a sunny day or to know where the North Star is at night.

2. Take your square of poster board, find the center and make a hole through it. About three hours before noon, go outside with your supplies and find a place that will get direct sunlight all day long. Carefully push the long, straight dowel through the hole in the poster board and into the ground so that the dowel points straight up. To make sure the dowel is *vertical*, tie a paper clip to one end of the string and hold it by the other end of the string near the dowel. The string will always hang vertically, so just make sure the stick is parallel to the string.

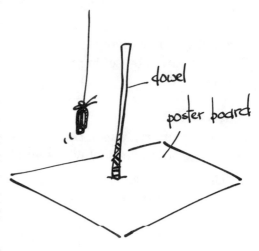

3. Now take the paper clip/string combination and slip the paper clip over the end of the dowel. Let it drop to the poster board base. Measure 12" of string from the paper clip and tie the loose end of the string to a pen or marker. Using the string as your radius, trace a circle with your pen by rotating the length of string around the base of the dowel. Take a quick peek at the drawing.

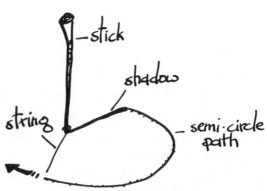

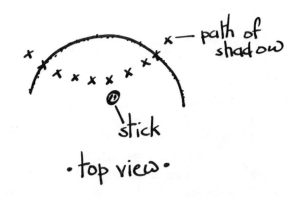

path of shadow

stick

·top view·

4. Look for the shadow cast by your dowel and mark where it ends on the cardboard. Make sure you record the time. (If you're on **Daylight Savings Time**, which runs from spring to fall, add one hour to the time you record. Why? The sun has no idea it's daylight savings time!) Check your stick's shadow every 15 or 20 minutes and mark the end of the shadow on your poster board. Keep track of the shadow's position and its corresponding time until about three hours after noon.

5. Drawing in a continuous arc, connect the positions you marked for your stick's shadow at different intervals of time. The arc that the shadow traces should intersect with the circle around the stick in two places.

6. Find the point on the shadow's path that's exactly *halfway* between where the shadow intersects the circle. Draw an arrow from the base of the stick to this point and you've found the direction of geographic north.

Explanation

You just marked the position of the stick's shadow for different times of the day. What you've created is your basic sundial. However, as a time piece, your "clock" will get worse and worse at telling the correct time as the year marches on. Six months from now, it'll be way off. The reason is that the earth is rotating and revolving around the sun and won't be in the same position for another year. But you can fix this problem by setting up your sundial so it's pointing in the same direction as the earth's north-south axis.

Procedure II

1. Take your clay, paper, pencil or pen, protractor, and triangular wedge out to the spot where you have the stick in the ground.

2. Using the clay, mount the triangular wedge perpendicular to the sheet of paper and aim it towards geographic north. You should know where north is because you figured that out earlier. Check out the drawing before you go any further.

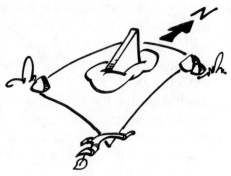

3. The wedge has to do two things: it has to point north and it has to line up exactly with the earth's axis. To do this, you need to know the latitude of where you live. You can find out your latitude from an atlas, a topographic map of your area, or by giving your favorite local radio or a TV station a call. If you can't locate your exact latitude, and you live in the United States, use 40 degrees north. Keep in mind that using the exact latitude will make your sundial more accurate.

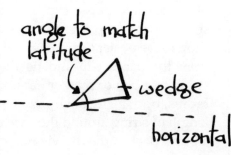

angle to match latitude

wedge

horizontal

4. Set up the triangular wedge so that its longest side is sloping "up" and is in line with north. It's angle with the paper must be the same as your latitude. Once you have the wedge lined up this way, it's called a **gnomon** (nó-mon).

5. Check your clock and start at about 9 AM. Mark on the paper the location of the tip of the gnomon's shadow every hour and label the times. Remember to add an hour if you're on daylight savings time. If you don't get sidetracked, do this for as many daylight hours as you have *time*.

6. If you kept track of your gnomon all day, and didn't move your equipment, you'll be able to tell the time by checking your sundial shadow. Remember that your gnomon and sundial are fragile so protect them from the weather.

More Explanation

The sun has always played a big part in history, religion, and science. For example, the ancient Egyptians had a sun god they called "Ra." With all that exposure, it's no surprise that clocks using shadows cast by the sun have been around since 3500 B.C. As long as you don't move them, sundials can also tell you more than just the time of day. They can be used like calendars and tell you what time of year it is. In summer, when the sun is high in the sky, the shadow is shorter than in winter when the sun is lower in the sky and the shadow is longer. For a real challenge, build a more permanent sun dial with weatherproof materials and record your sundial readings for a whole year. Then mark the dates that correspond to different shadow lengths.

Extension Ideas

1. Pick out a star or constellation (It might help to do this after dark, duh.) and watch it carefully as the night passes. You'll notice that the stars appear to move in a nice, regular pattern. Figure out how to make a "star dial" by recording the position of your star at different times. It's not an easy thing to do, because stars aren't in the same position at the same time on successive nights. Figure out how to correct for this.

2. The Egyptians used a shadow clock known as a **T-stick**. You can make a simple one by suspending a stick on top of two bricks or blocks of wood, as shown. By recording the position of the shadow cast by the stick at different times, you can tell time.

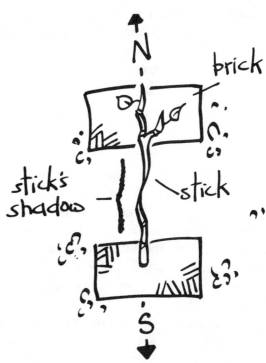

Science Fair Survival Techniques

On Your Own

Heat Wave - Cold Front

Materials

1 container of cold water	cooking oil
1 container of hot water	food coloring
1 index card	pen or pencil
1 length of tygon tubing	rubbing alcohol
1 rubber stopper, 1-hole	scissors
1 test tube	simple thermometer
clear tape	

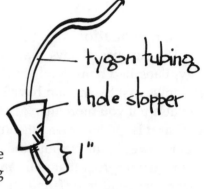

tygon tubing

1 hole stopper

1"

Procedure

1. Collect your instruments and head for the nearest sink. Push the tygon tubing through the 1-hole stopper until 1 inch of the tubing sticks out of the narrow end of the stopper.

2. Grab the test tube, and fill it completely with room-temperature water. Pick your favorite shade of food coloring and add a couple drops to the full test tube.

3. Push the narrow end of the rubber stopper, with attached tubing, into the test tube. Make sure the stopper fits tightly. The water should rise into the tubing. (This can be a messy procedure, so don't assemble it over the living room carpet.) Guess what, you just built a **thermometer**!

4. A couple more steps and clothing *faux pas* are a thing of the past because you'll always know the daily **temperature**. Now attach the index card. Hold it vertically, with the plain side facing you. Position it behind the tubing and set the bottom of the card on top of the stopper. Run the tubing up the center of the card and tape it in place. Cut off any excess tubing above the top of the index card. Later you'll mark the calibrations on the card.

5. Heat the test tube by placing it in a cup of very hot water. Notice when the water in the test tube heats up, the water begins to move up the tubing. Don't get the index card wet.

6. Grab your simple thermometer and use it to calibrate your homemade thermometer. Here's how. Place the simple thermometer into the cup of hot water along with the thermometer you just built. If the temperature on the simple thermometer rises to 120 degrees, then use a pen to make a 120 degree mark on the tubing and card of your thermometer. Your degree mark should be at the point where the water level settles in the tubing. Notice that the water settles in sort of a "U" shape. You should measure the liquid at the *bottom* of the "U" or the **meniscus** (mu-nís-kus). Next time you stick your thermometer into 120 degree water, the water level in the tube should rise to this mark.

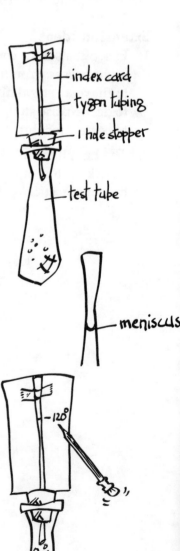

index card

tygon tubing

1 hole stopper

test tube

meniscus

120°

7. Try putting your thermometer into really cold water. Watch what happens to the water level in the plastic tubing. When the level in the tubing finally stops moving, you can calibrate the temperature again. Use the same method you used in Step #6.

8. Set your thermometer outside, in a vertical position and keep track of the temperature for a day or two. If you already have an outdoor thermometer, you can continue calibrating your thermometer by looking at the temperature and marking it at certain times of the day. Remember if you move the stopper in your thermometer, you'll have to start all over.

Explanation

Everyone knows what temperature is and what it feels like to be hot or cold. In order to understand why air feels a certain temperature, however, you have to think small. How small? As small as the zillions of invisible molecules that make up everything in our world including you, your friends, and your dog. Molecules are in constant motion. For example, there are air molecules playing bumper cars around you right now. You don't notice each time a molecule careens into you because they're so *tiny*. Besides there are tons of them smacking you around. What you do feel as a result of their movement is the sensation of temperature. If air molecules are hitting you really hard, then they give up some of their energy to the molecules in your skin, and the air feels *hot*. If the air molecules aren't moving very fast and they aren't hitting you as hard, the molecules in your skin give up some of their energy to the air, and the air feels *cool*. What all this means is that **temperature** is a measure of how fast molecules are moving.

The water molecules in your thermometer are in constant motion. As they get hotter, they move faster with more energy. To get more elbow room, they start to jostle around. This crazy activity causes the water to expand in the only direction it can, up the tubing. As the water cools, the molecules don't bump others as hard so they take up less space. This means the water goes back down the tubing.

Thermometers you buy at the store tell the temperature in many different ways. The liquid ones usually contain alcohol rather than water, because alcohol expands and contracts more than water when the temperature changes. Alcohol thermometers are sealed so the liquid doesn't evaporate. Some thermometers, like the outdoor "dial" type, rely on a piece of metal that expands and contracts with temperature changes. Liquid crystal thermometers are made of a series of different crystals that change their color at different temperatures. These thermometers are designed to have numbers that light up when a specific temperature is reached.

Extension Ideas

Try replacing the water in your thermometer with different liquids like cooking oil or rubbing alcohol. See which one makes the best thermometer.

Science Fair Survival Techniques

Take the Pressure

Materials

1 balloon
1 index card
1 pen or pencil
1 plastic bottle, 4 oz
1 rubber band
1 straw
   clear tape
   rock, optional
   scissors

Procedure

1. Cut the neck off the balloon and stretch the remaining part tightly over the top of the plastic bottle. To add weight to your bottle, you can put a rock in the bottom before covering it with the balloon. Seal the balloon to the bottle with a rubber band and some tape. Make sure you throw the other part of the balloon in the trash because in the wrong hands it can cause choking.

2. If your straw is wrapped, remove the wrapper, and lay the straw flat across the surface of the stretched balloon. Position and tape one end of the straw to the center of the stretched balloon.

3. Position the index card (white side facing you) lengthwise behind the bottle. Line up the base of the index card with the base of the bottle. Tape the index card in place.

4. On the index card, take a pen and mark the position of the taped end of the straw. What you've built is a **barometer**, which is something that measures changes in air pressure.

5. If there's a really tall building where you live, take your barometer there and ride up and down in the elevator. Notice what happens to the position of the end of the straw as you do this. No really tall building? Find a large mountain and convince someone to drive you up and down as you watch the straw. If you live in a flat place with no tall buildings or mountains, set your barometer on a table and watch the straw for a few days. You'll have to be patient though because you won't get much change unless a big storm passes through. If you live in tornado alley, you might get some serious pressure changes very quickly.

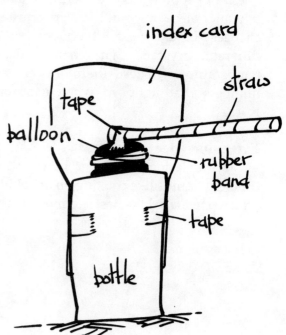

Explanation

So a **barometer** measures changes in **air pressure**. What exactly is air pressure? Remember those little air molecules moving around and bumping into things? You know, the ones that affect temperature? Well, they're also responsible for air pressure. The more molecules you have bumping into things and the harder they bump, the more air pressure they create. Fewer air molecules with a softer bump create less air pressure. Here's how your barometer works. When you first put it together, the air molecules inside the bottle and the air molecules outside the bottle push equally, so they have the same air pressure. If you change your altitude by climbing a mountain or going up in an elevator, the outside air pressure changes. That's because there are fewer air molecules at higher altitudes. Fewer air molecules means less air pressure. Meanwhile, the air pressure inside the bottle stays the same. If you reduce the outside air pressure but keep the inside pressure the same, the inside air pressure will "win out" and push the balloon piece upward. This causes the end of the straw to go down. Increasing the outside air pressure causes the balloon to be pushed in and the end of the straw will move up.

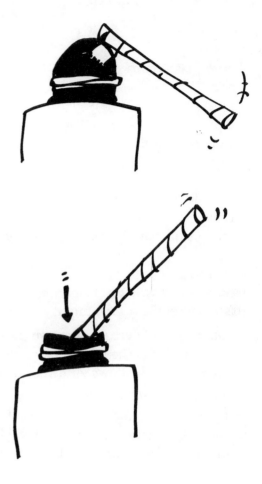

All right, so what does air pressure have to do with weather? Well, in certain parts of the world, very large **air masses** form that possess either *high* or *low* air pressure. Sometimes these masses can be huge and cover thousands of miles. High pressure areas are caused by air that starts from high in the atmosphere and sinks down to the earth's surface. Low pressure areas are caused by air that rises from the earth's surface towards the upper atmosphere. Since it's really hard for clouds and storms to form in sinking air, high pressure areas are places where the weather is usually pretty nice. On the other hand, it's easy for clouds and storms to form in rising air, so low pressure areas can be full of nasty weather.

High and low pressure areas move across the surface of the earth, creating different kinds of weather. Grab your local newspaper, or turn on the TV and check out the weather maps. In addition to all sorts of weird symbols that may look like hieroglyphics to you, you'll also see those big "H's" and "L's". These are the areas of high (**H**) and low (**L**) pressure. If you follow the maps for several days, you'll see that these H and L areas quite often move west to east across the United States.

On Your Own

Speedy Breezolas

Materials
    4 clear plastic cups
    2 straws
    1 push pin
    1 T-pin
    1 wooden dowel
        clear tape
        car and driver
        marker
        ruler
        scissors or sharp knife, with adult help

Procedure
1. Find an adult who can help you and ask them to bring a sharp knife or scissors with them. You might also want them to bring a ruler.

2. If you're good at eyeballing measurements, this will work fine, if not, use your ruler to find the middle of both straws, then make a small spot on the center of both straws with your marker.

3. Use your scissors or knife to cut a slit about a quarter of an inch long in the center of both sides of of the straws. Time to thread them together. No, not that way! Put the second straw through the slit in the first straw so that the two combined form a "+" sign.

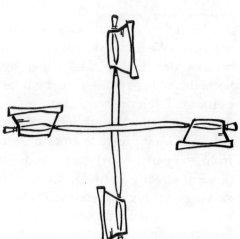

4. Take a plastic cup and use your scissors to cut two slits a quarter to half-inch long, directly across from each other, near the base of the cup. Repeat this for the other three cups.

5. Now you're going to slip the cups onto the straw cross through the slits you just made. You want to end up with something that looks like a water wheel. Look at the figure to make sure you get the direction of the cups on the straws correctly. Push the cups far enough onto the straws so that the straw end extends about a quarter-inch past the cup.

6. Bend the extended ends of the straws flat against the sides of the cups and tape them in place. This will keep them from falling off the straws.

7. Line up the center of the straws and use a push pin to poke a hole straight through both straws. Also use the push pin to make a hole in one end of the wooden dowel.

8. Push a "T" pin through the hole in both straws and then into the hole in the dowel. To help keep the two straws centered, you can use a piece of tape on either side of the straws at the intersection.

9. You did it amigo, you made a tool called an **anemometer** and it measures wind speed. If there's a wind blowing, take your anemometer outside and hold it by the dowel. The wind should cause the cups to spin. To make it easier to count each revolution, use a permanent marker to mark on the cups.

10. If there's no wind, try running with the anemometer and see if it spins. Make sure to watch where you're going. Duh!!

11. Time to calibrate your newest weather tool. Get someone to drive you in a car on a day when there's no wind. (It would be best to select an adult assistant with a driver's license for this part of the calibration.) As your assistant drives along, hold the anemometer out the window. Have your driver move along at 5 miles per hour while you count the number of turns the anemometer makes in one minute. Just count how many times the marked cup goes by you in one minute, and record that number. Then have your partner speed up to 10 miles per hour and repeat your count. Keep increasing the car's speed until the anemometer gets spinning so fast you can't count the turns anymore. Make sure your assistant doesn't break the speed limit. Once you have a set of numbers, you can mount your anemometer outside (maybe next to the weather vane) and use the number of turns per minute as an approximate measure of the *wind speed*.

Explanation

You probably already know that wind it's just a bunch of air moving from place to place, but what else do you know about wind?

Here's a way to help you get a grip on this wind notion. It's a breeze to figure it out.

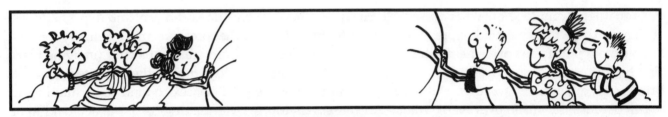

Imagine a big beach ball with three kids on both sides of the ball. If all the kids on both sides push equally hard on the ball, it's unlikely to move. However, if you take away kids from one side or the other, or if the kids on one side push harder than the kids on the other, the beach ball will move in a definite direction. Think of the kids as air molecules exerting pressure on the beach ball. There are two ways to move the beach ball:

Science Fair Survival Techniques

── On Your Own ─────────────────────

1. Decreasing the number of kids (air molecules) on one side decreases the air pressure on that side therefore, the ball moves toward the "low" pressure since the "high" pressure pushes it in that direction.

2. Having kids push harder on one side increases the air pressure on that side, so the higher (stronger) air pressure pushes the ball towards the lower (weaker) air pressure.

If high pressure areas push towards low pressure areas, one of the things that gets pushed is the air itself. All the air that's between a high pressure area and a low pressure area ends up being pushed towards the low pressure area. The air that gets pushed is **wind**.

Just to complicate things, it turns out that winds don't travel directly from highs (H) to lows (L). Since the earth is always spinning, there's a weird force called the **Coriolis Effect** which describes how winds travel in a curved path across the surface of our planet. The bottom line is that *winds tend to travel clockwise and downward around a high pressure area and counterclockwise and upward around a low pressure area, in the Northern Hemisphere.*

The boundary between a high and low is called a **front**. Winds tend to be very strong when you're at the *frontal edge* between a high and a low. You can expect winds to occur between those "H's" and "L's" as they move across the weather map. You might have heard your TV meteorologist talk about cold or warm fronts moving through your area.

You might want to know what causes it to be hot and humid some days and cool and dry other days. It all has to do with what kind of pressure area you're in and where that pressure area originally formed. An air mass that forms over the north pole tends to be a high pressure area that's cold (imagine that). The high pressure results in dry air. When this air mass moves across the northern United States, it brings cool or cold, dry weather. Air masses that form over the Gulf of Mexico tend to be humid and warm because they form over warm water. Air masses that form over the deserts of Mexico tend to be warm and dry. Something really interesting happens when different air masses run into each other, but you'll have to keep reading to find out that weather scoop.

Extension Ideas

Check the wind speed and direction daily for a couple of weeks. At the same time, check the weather map in your newspaper to see where the highs (H) and lows (L) are located. Watch for changes in wind direction as a storm front moves through your area. What wind do you expect when you're in the middle of a high pressure area? Start doing some of your own weather predictions and see how well you do.

Bumpin' Washers

Materials
6 metal washers
1 clear, wide-mouth jar
1 egg
1 paper tube
1 pie tin

Procedure

1. Find a smooth, slick surface to work on (your uncle's bald head isn't flat enough). Stack five of the washers on top of each other so they form a tower.

2. Set the remaining washer between you and the stack about 3 inches from the bottom. Aim at the base and give the lone washer a good hard flick with your finger toward the stack. What happens to the washer on the bottom of the stack when it gets hit? Where's the lone washer now? Repeat this several times to see if you get the same results.

3. Change the speed and the distance the washer is flicked at the stack. What happens? How could you shoot two washers? What happens with more or fewer washers in the stack? Try different sizes of washers.

4. Place one of the washers on a flat surface. Don't hit it, kick it, blow on it, tilt the surface, or budge it in any way. Just watch it and see if it starts moving all by itself. If you want to do a thorough job, keep watching for at least an hour. Your little brother might do this for you. Now, what's your conclusion?

Science Fair Survival Techniques

Explanation

Okay, let's start with a simple idea. Look at Item 4 in the *Procedure*. The washer just sitting by itself didn't move. If it did, you're living in the Bermuda Triangle. This simple observation illustrates a simple idea about the motion of things. It's half of Newton's First Law: Objects at rest want to remain at rest. If an object that's not moving suddenly starts moving, it's for sure that something hit it, shoved it, pushed it, pulled it, or otherwise gave it a whack (For the record, "pushes, pulls, shoves, whacks, etc." are the results of forces.). Think about the stack of washers. You can see why the bottom washer was pushed out from under the stack. The lone washer smacked it (exerted a force on it) and messed up its natural desire to stay at rest. The other washers in the stack didn't "feel" a thing. All they got was a new support washer underneath. They did what stationary objects do best: not move.

Extension Ideas

Let's use Newton's First Law to boggle somebody. Put a pie tin on top of a clear, wide-mouth jar full of water. Place an empty toilet paper tube in the center of the pie tin directly over the center of the jar. Place an egg point-first into the toilet paper tube and make sure it's centered over the jar. The only hard part is to make sure you hit, push, pull, smack, whack, or shove (any word that means applying a force) the tin solidly, quickly, and straight out from under the toilet paper tube. If everything is lined up, the tin and tube will zip to one side and the egg will drop into the jar of water (practice with a hard-boiled egg and graduate to a raw egg when you've got the hang of it). Since it's not moving, the egg wants to stay where it is, but its support has been knocked out from under it. Gravity says, "No way are you staying here!" and the egg is pulled straight down into the jar of water. A great use of Newton's First Law!

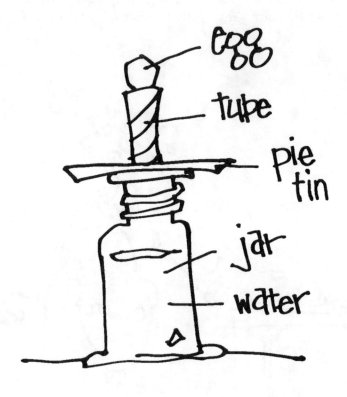

egg
tube
pie tin
jar
water

Gravity Puzzles and Projectiles

Materials
    6 wire ties, 2 different lengths (you might not use them all)
    2 ball bearings (any size or combination that fits the
        plastic tubing)
    1 card or paper, 3"x 5"
    1 length of plastic tubing, long
    1 piece of string
    1 partner to help
    1 stick of clay

Procedure

1. Let's look at a force that's so much a part of your life you probably ignore it. Use the clay to make two very different-sized balls — one very small and the other very large.

2. Hold the two balls side by side at the same height, say one meter, and drop them at the same time. Watch carefully and see which one hits the ground first. To win, one of the balls has to hit way before the other one. If it's close, you have to call it a tie.

   Now, try dropping the balls from a different height. Make note of the pattern that starts emerging after several trials. Try this with objects of various sizes and weights. Oh, it's probably a good idea not to use breakable things.

3. Now it's time to set up the tubing. First, try to anchor the string about 1.5 meters above the floor. That's tough to do so, be satisfied with anything around a meter high. Then tie the opening of the tubing so it is about a meter above the ground. Mount the rest of the tubing so that it gradually slopes downward with the last 10 cm of the tube positioned parallel to the floor and about 60 cm above it.

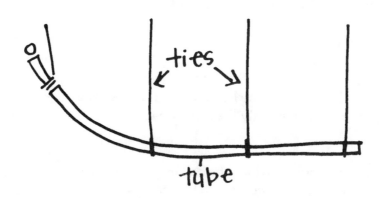

Science Fair Survival Techniques

4. Drop a ball bearing into the top of the tube. Watch it travel through the tube, shoot out, and land. Set the index card on the landing site to mark it and launch the ball again. Do this several times until it consistently lands in about the same place on the marker each time.

5. Have a partner stand next to the landing site with a second ball bearing. They should hold the bearing at exactly the same height as the exit hole of the tubing, but above the index card. This next part is sort of tricky. Drop the first ball bearing into the tubing. At the moment it emerges from the lower end, your partner should drop (not throw) the second ball bearing. You'll have to practice this a few times but based upon your experience with the clay, you should already be able to predict the results. To make sure, try dropping something much bigger and heavier than a ball bearing. How about a large rock or a brick? What results do you expect, now?

Explanation

When you dropped various objects side by side at the same time, which one hit first? The one in your left hand, perhaps? Trick question. They most likely landed about the same time. That's because gravity changed their speed and direction equally (gravity is really fair this way). However, if you tried a feather or piece of paper, you noticed they fell much slower. Wad or fold up the paper or crush the feather, test them again, and you'll see that gravity was working against air resistance but eventually won. After all, feathers are designed to stay in the air and a flat piece of paper has a lot of air resistance.

If you had the exit end of the tubing horizontal and your partner was able to drop the second ball just as the first ball emerged from the tube, you probably noticed that they hit the floor at about the same time. Maybe you expected it; maybe not. Remember "close" is a tie because of the very simple equipment you're using.

Think about what's going on. There is only one force acting on both of the balls — the gravitational pull of the earth. Gravity acts in a definite direction: toward the center of the Earth. The forward motion of the first ball is because of the shape of the tube. The ball is actually rolling downhill until it has no more support (tube) under it. Then, it stays in a forward motion (First Law) while being forced toward the earth by gravity. It stops only when it hits the ground. The second ball has no motion (it's at rest) until it has no support (your partner let go) and then gravity starts forcing it downward. If gravity is the only force acting on the balls that are at the same height, then they'll change their speed and direction at exactly the same rate and hit the Earth at exactly the same time.

Extension Ideas

1. Experiment with increasing the angle at which the ball bearing leaves the tube. In other words, raise the opening. See if you can discover the best angle that causes the ball to go as far as possible.

2. See what happens when you change the height of the tubing entrance and the angle at which the bearing shoots out.

Balloon Rockets

Instruments:
    1 balloon
    1 long piece of string
    1 small spring
    1 straw
        tape

Procedure

1. Look for a solid base about eye level that won't move when one end of a string's tied to it. It's easiest if you get someone to hold the free end when you do this experiment. However, you can do this by yourself if you work at the free end of the string.

2. Unwrap the straw and thread it onto the free end of the string. Slide it down to the fixed end if you have a helper. If you're working solo, keep the straw with you at the free end.

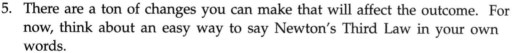

3. Blow up the balloon but don't tie it off. Just pinch it for now. Use two pieces of tape to hold the inflated balloon to the straw. Attach the balloon so that the "nozzle" end is pointing toward the closest anchor. For now, it helps to have the balloon, straw, and string all parallel to each other. If you're alone, you have to pinch the nozzle while you do all this. Yes, you have to be fairly coordinated, but you'll get it with practice.

4. Have your helper (or you if it's lonesome) hold on to the free end of the string, pull it tight, and make sure it's more-or-less level. Release the balloon. Enjoy, and no screaming, please. Practice this launch several times to get the hang of it and to make the balloon move smoothly up the string.

5. There are a ton of changes you can make that will affect the outcome. For now, think about an easy way to say Newton's Third Law in your own words.

Explanation

The balloon rocket accelerated (velocity changed), right? Absolutely! So, you know a force was exerted on it and it moved away from you along the string. Here's an interesting thought: forces applied to an object must come from outside the object. In other words, an object can't push or pull itself. Question: What did the pushing in the case of the rocket? The answer is taken, of course, from Newton's Third Law: when an object is pushed, it pushes back with an equal force. You push on a wall, it pushes back. A rock hits you on the head, your head hits back with an equal force (but, ow, it hurts!). A truck runs into a car, the car pushes back on the truck with an equal force (With what you know about mass and inertia, you can explain why the car is damaged more than the truck.).

Some folks have a hard time with this action/reaction idea so try this as a convincer: Get a small spring. Hold it in one hand and squeeze it (see the diagram).

Does the spring push back? Of course it does, it's a spring. You push, it pushes back. Now, imagine you're pressing on a whole set of springs, like the box springs that are under the mattress on your bed.

Do the springs push back? Sure do. Ever wonder why? Let's make these springs stiffer and stiffer, so they barely move unless you push really hard on them. Do they still push back? Yes, but it's hard to detect. You can use this as a pretty good model of how walls and other solid objects push back when pushed upon. Solid objects (like everything else) are built of molecules connected by "stiff springs." (They're not really springs, but it helps to understand it better if you think of it that way.) Push on molecules, they push back. So, if you believe that even stiff springs push back, maybe you'll believe that walls, rocks, and other objects push back when pushed on, too.

Where does the balloon rocket fit into all this? You can now explain its motion as follows. When you let go of the balloon, it wanted to get back to its smaller size. In the process, the balloon squished the air (gas) inside and shoved it out the nozzle. The gas pushes on the object and . . . Voila!. . . . object is accelerated forward. Keep in mind, though, it's quite a bit more complicated than just that. But, how do you like being a beginning rocket scientist?

Running the Rapids

What types of repulsion are there? Mother Nature always has new ways for us to view our world. In this experiment, you're going to ponder polarity and its relationship to repulsion.

Materials

1 glass of water	cooking oil
1 test tube	sodium chloride (table salt)

Procedure

1. Grab the test tube, the bottle of cooking oil, and then get a glass of cold tap water.

2. Take a look at the water you're holding in the glass. Describe all you can about it. Taste it (only if you're sure it's clean and fresh).

3. Fill ¼ of the test tube with the cooking oil and recap the bottle. Describe the oil as you did the water. What differences do you see? How are they the same? Taste it (if you want to) and describe it.

4. Slowly add water "on top" of the oil until the test tube is ¾ full. You now have ½ the volume of the test tube filled with water and ¼ of it filled with oil. What happened to the oil on the bottom of the test tube when the water was added?

5. Use your thumb as a stopper for the test tube and shake the test tube like crazy. Stop shaking and watch what happens. Describe what you see. How long does it take to re-form two layers? What if you use hot water?

6. After everything settles down, open the bottle of sodium chloride (table salt) and sprinkle a little bit into the test tube. Watch what happens to the salt. After you think you know what's going on, give the test tube another shake to speed up the process that you see.

salt

water

oil

test tube

Explanation

So, let's take a deeper look at the tiny foundation of science...the atom. Unless you're going to talk about really tiny things (subatomic particles), then the atom is the basic building block of everything. Atoms pile up together in certain ways and form molecules. Chemists classify molecules into general groups to study and analyze (groups like inorganic, organic, biochemical, and organometallic, just to name a few). All these different groups promote considerable argument as to which field of chemistry is the "purest" form of science. (Let's not even mention the physicists' point of view!) In spite of all this discussion, the one thing they can agree upon is that you can't live without one particular compound. It's a simple, yet complex molecule, truly in a glass by itself, a solvent among solvents, able to satisfy those who thirst for knowledge. Yes, it's water — fresh, clear, clean, distilled, deionized Type II water. Water is an interesting molecule. It's called a **polar** molecule (as in positive and negative, **not** north and south) because its electrons are not evenly distributed throughout the molecule. They sort of like to hang out on one side of the molecule and that creates a negative charge on that side. The opposite side of the molecule winds up being more positive.

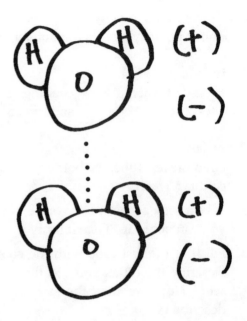

If you look at water more closely, you can see what's happening. Water is made up of three atoms: two tiny hydrogen and one huge oxygen (written as H_2O in chem-ese). The molecule is kind of bent with the big oxygen atom in the middle connected (bonded) to the two tiny hydrogen atoms. They're pointing away from it at an angle kind of like the outline of Mickey Mouse's head. The oxygen atom has "a thing" for electrons. It says, "I want more electrons!" (electronegative) and tries to coax them into coming over to it.

On the other hand, hydrogen says, "Great, take mine!" (electropositive) and freely gives up its single electron to the oxygen atom. The result is the oxygen side of a water molecule is more negative and the hydrogen side is more positive. Voila! . . . a polar molecule. Thus, water molecules attract each other with "electrical" interactions. The positive side of one molecule attracts the negative side of another molecule, whose positive side grabs onto someone's negative side, and, . . . well, you get the picture.

Oil is **nonpolar**. Its electrons are evenly distributed across the molecule. So it doesn't have any attraction for polar molecules like water. This means that water molecules attract each other because they're polar, but there's <u>no</u> attraction of nonpolar oil and polar water molecules. So, oil and water don't mix; they can't **dissolve** in each other.

The reason oil *floats* on top of the water is due to the fact that oil is less **dense** than water. Since everyone in the world can get water, it's used as the reference density for everything else. Water was given a density of 1.00 grams per milliliter. Corn oil, for instance, has a density of about 0.92 grams per milliliter and linseed oil is around 0.93 grams per milliliter. Both are less than that of water, so they float on top of it.

The salt you sprinkled on the oil (which was on top of the water) eventually broke the **surface tension** of the oil and fell through both liquids to the bottom of the test tube. This means that salt has to be more dense than oil *or* water. Salt's density is about 2.17 grams per milliliter — that's more than *twice* as dense as water.

The salt also **dissolved** in the water. Yep! You guessed it. Salt is a **polar molecule.** It is made up of just two atoms: sodium (Na) and chlorine (Cl). Salt is also **ionic**, in that the sodium metal always likes to be positively charged (Na^+) and the chlorine nonmetal always likes being negatively charged (Cl^-). When combined like this, sodium chloride is polar-ionic having positive and negative sides, like water. Like dissolves like, so, it dissolves in water very nicely, thank you.

Extension Ideas

1. When most things get cold, they contract (get smaller). If you freeze water, does it expand or contract? What about oil or vinegar? Water is unique in that it expands when it becomes a solid. There are at least nine different forms of ice. Where do they come from and how are they formed?

   Find out what you can about "solid water."

2. Consider this: the frozen form of most liquids <u>sinks</u> (higher density). Solid water <u>floats</u> on itself. Dig in and find out why and then ask, "How would life on earth change if ice *didn't* float?"

117

Suds and Duds

How can you dissolve oil in water? Here's a question many teenagers deal with as they apply all that oily stuff to their hair. Perhaps you've tried to clean greasy hamburger drool off of your shirt. Fortunately, soap comes to your rescue. Let's see what happens to oil and water when soap's in the neighborhood.

Materials
    1 test tube, or a clear glass
    1 glass of water
        cooking oil
        liquid soap

Procedure
1. Get a glass of cold tap water and fill the test tube or clear tumbler ½ full.

2. Open a bottle of liquid soap and add several drops to the tube (about ½ ml). Watch them fall to the bottom of the water. It's cool the way they stream down.

3. Use your thumb to cap the end of the test tube and vigorously shake it up and down. What do you see? Look at the water layer and the foam layer. Note the size and number of bubbles in each location. Watch for 5 minutes and note the changes you see.

4. Rinse out your test tube and fill it ½ full with fresh water.

5. Open the bottle of cooking oil and pour some into the test tube with the water until it is ¾ full. Recap it!

6. Cap the test tube with your thumb again, and shake the contents. You should have a good idea what's going to happen if you did the previous experiment. Let the liquids separate and note the changes in them.

7. Open your soap bottle and add the same amount as before to the test tube. Lids on! Cover the test tube with your thumb and start shaking. Ten seconds later, describe what you see. If you need to, add more soap and shake again.

soap

water

oil

test tube

Explanation
Soap is part of a group of compounds called **surfactants** [sir-fac'-tents] or surface-active agents. Soap molecules mess up the surface tension of water and that results in all those suds you saw. The action of shaking also forced air into the soap-water mixture creating the foam. All that foam shows another property of surfactants — a little bit goes a long way. It doesn't take very much to cover a large surface area when your soap layer is only about one molecule in thickness.

When the oil and water mixture was shaken, blobs of oil were mechanically dispersed throughout the water. They couldn't dissolve in each other (polarity difference) and the oil returned to the top (density difference). To overcome these differences, a third party has to be called on to help. Yes, none other than soap!

Soap molecules have a polar (**hydrophilic**—water loving) end which attracts water molecules. There's also a nonpolar (**hydrophobic**—fear of water) end which attracts oils and dirt. Soap's surfactant action lowers the surface tension of the water. This helps to dislodge dirt and oils from large surface areas. When the soap is added to the oil and water mixture and shaken, an **emulsion** (suspension) of oil in water forms. The soap molecules grabbed the oil molecules with their hydrophobic ends and held onto the water molecules with their hydrophilic ends.

Extension Ideas

1. Fill a bowl with cool water and "float" a needle on the water's surface. There are several ways to do this. One is to lay the needle on a small piece of tissue and carefully lay the tissue on the surface of the water. Using a toothpick, gently push the tissue down and away from the needle until the tissue sinks and the needle "floats" on the surface. This may take several tries but it's worth it. The surface tension of the water is strong enough that the needle will seem to float just like a canoe. Dip your toothpick in some soap and barely touch the surface of the water somewhere in the dish. If a little bit of soap touches the surface of the water, the surface tension will be broken and the floating needle will fall to the bottom. Try and float another needle on this same batch of water. Good luck. You'll discover the staying power of a surfactant. Give up? Try fresh water.

2. Here's a tough one: how does the absorption and/or excretion of medicines in the body relate to whether they're hydrophobic or hydrophilic?

Gas It Up

How could a gas be dissolved in a liquid? If you're a fish or other aquatic animal, this is a very important question. What about those bacteria that sour milk? Do they need to breathe? What about bad breath? How does a soda pop get its fizz? Questions, questions, questions. Let's begin by looking at how gas dissolves in liquids.

Materials
    1 glass of water
    1 test tube or clear glass
    1 thumb
        acetic acid(vinegar)
        cooking oil
        sodium bicarbonate (baking soda)
        sodium chloride (table salt)

Procedure

1. It's observation time! Nab a test tube and fill it ⅓ full with water. Cap the tube with your thumb and shake the tube or stir the water. Look very closely at the air bubbles you mechanically trap in the water while you shake and afterwards. How quickly do they rise to the surface of the water when you stop? What if you try hot water?

2. Pour out the water and refill ⅓ of the tube with cooking oil. Cap and shake again. Compare the rising speed of these bubbles to the ones in water.

3. Pour the oil back into its bottle and recap the bottle. Wash out the test tube with some soap and water. Hmmmm, why do you need to use soap to clean it out, anyway (see *Suds and Duds*)?

4. Place about ¼ teaspoon of sodium bicarbonate in the test tube. Recap the bottle. Over a small dish, pour an equal amount of the acetic acid into the test tube. Describe what happened. Compare the foams you've made: How long do they last? What size are the bubbles? What changes do you see?

5. After all the fizzing has stopped, recap the acetic acid and get out your sodium chloride.

6. When the fizz is nearly gone, sprinkle some salt into the test tube. What happened? Add some more. What happened this time? When you're done, cap it and clean it!

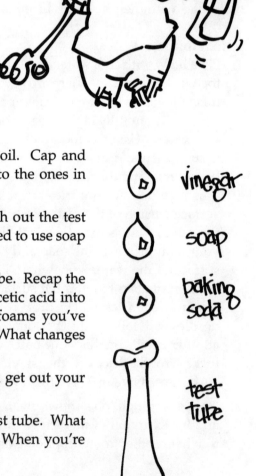

vinegar

soap

baking soda

test tube

Explanation

Air is only slightly soluble in either oil or water. When oil or water is vigorously shaken, a mechanical dispersion of air occurs in them. Gas bubbles travel to the surface of the liquids because of their lower density. The rising speed of bubbles in a liquid depends on the viscosity (how runny it is) of the liquid; either rapidly, as in water, or more slowly, as in the oil.

When acetic acid (vinegar) is mixed with sodium bicarbonate (baking soda solution), carbon dioxide gas is produced. Carbon dioxide gas is partially soluble in water and forms carbonic acid. Even after the fizzing has stopped, this acid occupies space in between the water molecules. It can be driven out of this space by adding another water soluble substance. You used sodium chloride or plain old table salt. Being a water soluble molecule, salt dissolves in water and actually pushes the gas out of the space so it bubbles to the surface.

Extension Ideas

1. Sodium bicarbonate is often used as an antacid and leavening agent in cooking. How does sodium bicarbonate help people with indigestion and how does it make foods taste better so they get indigestion in the first place? Ask an adult.

2. Now that you know that carbon dioxide can dissolve in water, look into the process of photosynthesis and explore the idea of the exchange of oxygen and carbon dioxide in plants . . . especially those in the ocean. How deep can plants live under water? What limits their range? How do they receive sunlight? What about oxygen? Lots of questions here. It's a big body of water!

Hey Copper

And the Current Question Is?

Why is copper sulfate blue and not copper-colored? Good question! Copper sulfate is a salt of copper metal, which means that the copper atoms are ionized having a positive (+2) charge. The charge on copper changes its electronic shape (how its electrons are oriented around the nucleus) so that when light hits the copper sulfate, a blue color is seen rather then a copper color. Using electricity, you can change the copper ion (Cu^{+2}) to copper metal. It's a process that's been around for almost 200 years! Let's do it, too!

Materials

2 insulated wires	1 pair of latex gloves
1 battery, D-cell	1 nail
1 cup of water	copper sulfate

Procedure

1. The first thing you need to do is put on your latex gloves to protect your fingers. Then pour about two capfuls of copper sulfate into the cup of water. Stir the solution to help the crystals dissolve. If they all dissolve, add another capful and stir again. Recap the bottle when you're finished.

2. Strip about 2 cm of insulation off of both ends of the wires. Take one of the wires and wrap a stripped end around the nail so that it makes a good connection with the nail. Immerse the entire nail in the copper sulfate solution. Let the other end dangle over the edge of the cup for now. Take a second wire and simply immerse one of its ends in the solution. Make sure the second wire doesn't touch the nail. Its other end can dangle over the edge of the cup for now, too.

3. Check out the battery. It has a positive and a negative terminal. Take both dangling ends of the wires and connect them to the terminals of the battery by pinching them between your fingers and the battery. Make sure the wire from the nail is connected to the negative (-) side (that's the flat end) and the loose wire is connected to the positive (+) side (the one with a knob on it). When the last connection is made, look at a clock and time what you see. Watch the nail closely. How long did it take to completely electroplate the nail?

battery
wires
glass
copper sulfate
nail

Explanation

Electroplating is the process that deposits one kind of metal onto another kind of metal. Copper sulfate is called an **electrolyte** because it can break into smaller "pieces" (the copper and sulfate **ions** Cu^{+2} and SO_4^{-2}) and conduct electricity. As electricity is passed through the blue copper sulfate solution it produces a chemical change (**electrolysis**). You used the battery to "push" the copper ions within the solution to the iron nail.

Copper ions are carried to the nail (the cathode) from the loose copper wire (the anode). The electricity reduces the copper ion to simple copper metal and electricity "plates" it onto the nail's surface. In this process (electroplating), it's best to make sure the anode is made of the same metal as that which is being taken from a solution. This makes it possible to replace the metal in solution with the same metal from the anode. This means that if copper is being plated, then use a copper solution and a copper anode.

Extension Ideas

1. Try this same process, only dissolve the copper sulfate in vinegar instead of water. If you're really ambitious, get some other metal salts for electroplating, like silver nitrate or nickel sulfate. How do you think gold plating might work? How do you bronze your baby shoes?

2. Here are some other ideas you may want to try. How does the process change if you use a weaker or stronger battery? How about trying more than one battery? Look around for other metals to try in the copper sulfate solution. Suppose you try moving the loose wire closer to and farther from the nail. How do your results change if the cathode and anode touch? What happens if the nail becomes the anode?

On Your Own

Electric Symphony

What other materials conduct electricity? Just look around you. There are so many electrons whizzing about you that if you could see them all, you'd be dizzy. They're everywhere and they keep the world moving. So, grab your baton and join the great "conductors" of the Electric Symphony. After all, you wouldn't want to "insulate" you from some culture.

Materials
    2 insulated wires
    1 battery
    1 light bulb and socket

Procedure

1. Connect one end of each of the two wires to a separate screw on the light bulb socket. Screw in the light bulb. The free ends can just dangle. Why isn't the bulb glowing, yet?

2. Test your set up by holding the loose ends of the two wires to a separate terminal of the battery with your fingers. Did the light go on? If not, make sure the contacts are solid and the bulb is OK and try again. If it works, you're off and rolling. Isn't the suspense "electrifying"?

3. OK, now you have your Test Unit. Walk around and test for things that will conduct electricity. Do this by placing the test object between the positive (+) terminal of the battery and the loose end of the wire from the light. The other wire goes from the light to the negative (-) terminal which is probably under your thumb.

4. Keep a list of the materials that lit the bulb and those that didn't. The test objects you used that didn't cause the bulb to light are called insulators. If the bulb glowed, you were testing a conductor.

Explanation

When you're talking electricity, there are four basic groups of materials: insulators, conductors, semi-conductors, and superconductors. A **conductor** is a chunk of matter (solid, liquid, gas) that allows electrons to move through it. In other words, electricity flows through the object. Most metals are conductors. In the previous experiment, you also found that electrolytes in solution can conduct electricity. This means electrons move through these electrolytic solutions using ions for their transportation.

An **insulator** is just the opposite. It *prevents* the passage of electrons through it. **Semiconductors** have properties of both conductors and insulators. Silicon and germanium are elements used in semiconductors. They are sometimes called **metalloids** because they have conductive properties of both metals and non-metals.

Some conductors move electrons better than others. Many of them "don't like" having these bundles of energy move through them and they "resist" it. This resistance to moving electrons creates heat due to friction. This heat may cause an electrical fire because a conductor is trying to carry too many electrons all at once. Superconductors, however, have no electrical resistance. There is no heat generated and electric currents can flow through the superconducting material forever without any loss of energy.

Extension Ideas

1. Try this experiment with a different battery. Use a 6-volt battery. With the added voltage, you should be able to test different solutions for conductivity. Test salt water, vinegar, distilled water, or lime water. By the way, when you connect the circuit through the light bulb, why does it produce light? Since you're talking about light, how does a laser work?

2. See if you can locate an ohm meter. It can accurately measure the **resistance** of different materials in units called the ohm. Is there a coincidence in the name of the meter? Just for the heck of it, metals usually have a resistance between 1×10^{-6} and 1×10^{-5} ohms/meter; semiconductors between 1×10^{-6} and 1×10^{8} ohms/meter; and, insulators between 1×10^{7} and 1×10^{17} ohms/meter. What would your ohm meter show for the resistance of a superconductor?

3. Learn more about electronics, the semiconductor industry, computers, and superconductors. They're rapidly expanding fields of knowledge!

Talk About Charisma

What are some properties of magnets? Good question. A **lodestone** (a mineral now called magnetite) was the first permanently magnetic material discovered. That was way back during the time of the ancient Greeks. They mined the lodestone in a district named Magnesia which is where the name "magnet" is thought to have originated. It wasn't too long after lodestone was studied that a compass was invented, people realized the earth spun on its axis, and the Boy Scouts had a reason to go camping. What's drawn to a magnet? What is magnetic force? Above all, why are they found on refrigerators? Isn't applied science fun!

Materials
2 ring magnets
1 adult helper
1 pencil
1 TV set

Procedure
1. Pick up your ring magnets and investigate different objects like spoons, books, tables, doorknobs, glass, wood, or almost anything you see. Stay far away from televisions, computers and storage discs, video recorders and tapes, camera equipment, and cassette tapes. *Magnetic fields will damage these items!*

2. Use the pencil to make a list of everything that was attracted to the magnets as well as those that weren't.

3. The first thing you should do for this one is find an adult that can help. It's not that this is a difficult lab, just that you wouldn't want to damage the TV. Turn on your television, but make sure the magnets are at least three meters away from the set.

4. When the picture has appeared, slowly bring the magnets toward the picture tube until you see a change in the image. Don't touch the magnets directly to the glass and don't go closer than is necessary to see the initial effects (about 50 cm). The picture will begin to get distorted and may show different colorations with the magnet close by. Magnets can damage the picture quality by changing the focus of the electron beam. This means that whenever you watch the tube, you might have a bright red spot in the middle of the screen that will never go away. That is, until you call a TV repair man, pay some big bucks, and apologize to everyone. So be very careful!

Explanation

The materials that you found to be **magnetic** usually have some iron in them. However, cobalt, nickel, gadolinium, and a few other metals exhibit magnetic properties as well. Other materials like wood, glass, rubber, plastic, cloth, aluminum, copper, and other items do not display magnetic attraction.

In order to answer the question as to what makes them magnetic, you need to look right at the atom. Each "electron layer" (orbital) around the nucleus of an atom likes to have two electrons. If all the electrons are there, then it is **diamagnetic**. That means that it *repels* a magnetic field. This **repulsion** is so slight that you can't even feel it. Gold, copper, silver, plastic, water, cloth — these are all diamagnetic. They are <u>not</u> attracted to the magnet.

If a couple of electrons are missing from the inner "layers" of an atom, then the atom is said to be paramagnetic. Some of the electrons no longer have a partner. Things in this group act like they have lots of little magnets (dipoles) that are all disorganized. When the item is brought near a magnetic field, the dipoles line up in proper order. This is kind of like bringing a magnet next to a group of compasses and seeing all the needles point toward the magnet. When the item is inside a magnetic field, it becomes a magnet itself and is attracted toward the field.

Ferromagnetism is associated with those materials that stay magnetic in the absence of a magnetic field. Iron is an example of an element that is both ferromagnetic as well as paramagnetic. At high "critical" temperatures, like **1292°F**, the iron atoms shift their electrons becoming paramagnetic, losing their permanent magnetic quality. At lower temperatures, the iron atoms become ferromagnetic and can maintain their own magnetic field. The ring magnets in this kit are examples of iron compounds that are ferromagnetic (they stay magnetized).

When the magnet was brought toward, not touching, the television, a lot of distortion occurred. Why? Remember that whenever there are moving electrons, a magnetic field is generated. When the TV is turned on, the picture forms by the projection of electrons (moving particles) onto the glass surface. The surface is coated with a chemical compound (phosphor) that converts the electron energy into visible, radiant light: the picture you see. If the electrons are moving, they must have a magnetic field. When you brought the ring magnets toward the picture tube, the electrons were attracted toward the magnet and pulled out of alignment distorting the picture.

Extension Ideas

1. Find out how the electron beam is formed and focused in a television. Look into different recording media like video tapes, compact disks, wire recorders, and computer hard drives to see what makes them tick.

2. If you really want to look at some high tech stuff, check into nuclear magnetic resonance and magnetic resonance imaging used in the medical field.

Science Fair Survival Techniques

── On Your Own ───────────────────

Let There Be Light

Ever notice how the tree outside a window makes huge, soft shadows on the wall? The effect is created by the way the light bends around the leaves and branches. In this activity, you'll learn about how and why this happens and how hard and soft shadows are created. Then you can make your own special effects.

Materials

1 flashlight	cellophane tape
1 paper tube	eyebrow pencil
1 sheet of aluminum foil	hand-held mirror
1 sheet of plain paper	pencil or pen
1 small toy figurine	scissors
a dark room or closet	

Procedure

1. Trace the picture of the branch and leaves onto your piece of paper. Cut it out. So far, so good.

2. Take the flashlight, toy figure, leaf cut-out, and yourself into a dark room or closet. Your shins will probably thank you if you use the light.

3. Project a shadow of the figure onto the wall. Now, experiment a bit with the arrangement. Put the figure close to the flashlight and far from the wall and vice versa. Make any changes you can think of to alter the shadow. Notice the different kinds of shadows you get.

4. Repeat #3 with the leaf cut-out. As you do this, think about how you might use the different kinds of shadows for different effects on a stage. Think like a lighting director.

Explanation

When you place an object in the path of a beam of light, it casts a shadow behind it. Duh. Okay, that's easy enough but there's more to a shadow than merely blocking light. For instance, the shadow that you see when you're standing in the sun is pretty much always the same. Well, its size and shape change as the sun changes position or you move, but it pretty much looks the same all the time. With the flashlight and a small object, however, you can create sharp, clear shadows, fuzzy shadows, light shadows, dark shadows, big shadows, little shadows, etc. The main reason for the difference is that light from the sun (93 million miles away) is traveling in about the same direction. Light from a flashlight quickly spreads out in just a few feet. Compare the size of the flashlight spot when it's close to the wall with the size of the spot when it's far away from the wall.

Shadows are also affected by how much light bends around an object. You might have heard that light always travels in straight lines, but that isn't exactly true. The fancy schmancy name for light bending around a corner or an edge of something is **diffraction**. If you hold an object close to the light but far from a surface, the light that bends around the object's edges tends to get mixed up in the shadow and the shadow looks fuzzy and gray. Far from a light but close to a surface makes dark, precise shadows.

You can use all this knowledge about shadows to create special effects on stage. Want to project the shadow of a "mysterious stranger" on stage? Move the person closer to a surface so the audience can tell it's a person's shadow. Want "scary monster" shadows? Then you're better off with fuzzy shadows that come from putting the monster closer to the light source and further from the surface. Let the audience use some imagination.

Procedure

1. Take two smooth sheets of aluminum foil and the flashlight into your dark room.

2. Either hold a piece of the foil or set it down on something. Shine the flashlight at it so the light reflects off the foil and onto a surface. Study the reflection carefully because you're about to be tested.

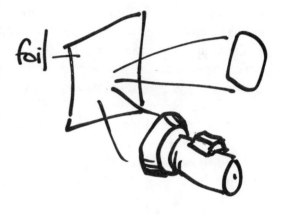

3. Crinkle up the other piece of foil slightly, unfold it part way, and repeat Step #2. Compare what you see now with what you can see from the smooth piece. What's going on here?

4. Now you're going to get help you with something that might have been bugging you already. Have you noticed that the spot made by the flashlight is brighter at its center and there's all sorts of designs and stuff around it? To change (improve?) things, put a layer of cellophane tape across the end of the flashlight (preferably the end the light comes out). Cover the entire endcap and shine it on the wall. Vive la différence!

5. What? Not happy yet? You say the light spreads out too much, now? No problemo. Tape the paper tube to the tape-covered flashlight, as shown, and shine it on the wall again.

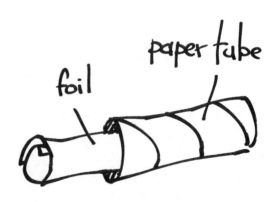

6. One last technique to explore. Take your smooth aluminum foil from Step 3 and line the inside of the paper tube with it. Roll it into a tube slightly smaller than the paper tube, place it inside, and then unroll it so it fits against the inside wall.

7. Put this tube on the flashlight and see what you get when you shine it on the wall. Try it with and without the cellophane tape over the endcap. Create some shadows with it and test your new lighting equipment.

— On Your Own —

More Explanation

For you, a simple flashlight begins the process of getting light where you want it, how you want it, and when you want it. You now have a few tricks to put into your stage-lighting repertoire. The key to these tricks is getting the light to do what you want it to do. By crumpling the aluminum foil, you create not one, but hundreds of surfaces off of which the light reflects. This leads to interesting multiple shadows.

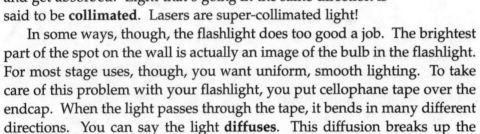

The light produced by the bulb spreads out in all directions. The reflective surface behind and on the sides of the bulb helps get the light moving in generally the same direction. The trouble is that this reflecting surface is kind of cheap and doesn't do such a great job of sending the light in the same direction. That's why the light spreads out so much. The paper tube partly takes care of that. Only the light rays headed straight out anyway make it out the tube. Light that isn't headed straight forward tends to hit the sides of the tube and get absorbed. Light that's going in the same direction is said to be **collimated**. Lasers are super-collimated light!

In some ways, though, the flashlight does too good a job. The brightest part of the spot on the wall is actually an image of the bulb in the flashlight. For most stage uses, though, you want uniform, smooth lighting. To take care of this problem with your flashlight, you put cellophane tape over the endcap. When the light passes through the tape, it bends in many different directions. You can say the light **diffuses**. This diffusion breaks up the reflected image and results in light that spreads evenly over the surface.

With the diffusion from the cellophane tape and the collimation from the foil-lined paper tube, you have a reasonably good spotlight. Of course real spotlights are a bit more complex. They use adjustable lenses to change the size of the spot and something brighter than a flashlight for a light source!

Extension Ideas

Using light reflections and shadows, you can create cool illusions and special effects. Here are a few to try.

1. Go in a dark room with a mirror. Look in the mirror, shine the flashlight on your face from the side, and notice what kind of shadow your nose casts. Keeping the light where it is, bend your nose slightly so it looks like it's broken. Notice the shadow now. Use the eyebrow pencil to draw the "broken nose shadow" on your face. Shine the flashlight straight on your face and see if it looks a wee bit like you have a broken nose. Actual make-up techniques are much more complex than this, but this is a start.

2. Back in your dark room, try shining your homemade spotlight on the doll or action figure from different angles. From below-front is a common lighting angle for scary scenes. Lighting from the back is called "back lighting" (no brainer) and creates a halo effect. This is used to really focus attention on the person in the light and make them look "bigger than life." You can also experiment with different lighting angles on your own face as you look into a mirror. Hey, it's your chance to shine — as it were.

Color Your Thinking

Color comes in waves. Splash some on a stage!

Materials

6 colored acetates (gels)	adult help
3 flashlights	cellophane tape
3 paper tubes	scissors
1 pencil	white surface

Procedure

1. You're going to make three spotlights that mix colors. Find an adult to help you with this step. Start by cutting two-thirds of the way through each tube about an inch from the end. Try to make it as even a cut as possible.

2. Set a tube in a corner of one of the colored gels as shown and trace the outline of half the tube's circumference. Cut the gel as shown. To begin with, it's better to start by cutting the gel a little too big and then trim as necessary. It's the old "measure twice, cut once" rule.

3. Slide the cut gel into the gap in one of the tubes as shown. If it stays where it is and covers the entire inside of the tube (no white light leaks), use this gel as a pattern and cut the others the same way. You're looking for a snug fit but with no wrinkles in the gel. It's snug but the gel should slide easily in to and out of the gap. If you need to trim it slightly, don't cut too much at a time and test it after each cut.

4. Set up your spotlights as you did in the previous activity. Be sure to cover each flashlight endcap with cellophane tape and the cut paper tubes are taped onto the flashlight with the gel end away from the flashlight. You may want to use the aluminum foil liner, too. Each flashlight is now a spotlight that can produce any color of light you want if you have the gel. Simply slide different gels into the gap in the tube to change colors.

5. Take your spotlights and gels into that closet or dark room you've been in so much recently. If the room has white walls, you're in business. If not, you'll need something white for your lights. A piece of paper will do nicely.

6. Shine combinations of two colors (using two spotlights) onto the white surface and figure out what combinations lead to what colors. For example, what happens when a red spotlight combines with a yellow spotlight?

131

7. Record the combinations below.

<u>red</u> and <u>yellow</u> make _____

_____ and _____ make _____

_____ and _____ make _____

_____ and _____ make _____

_____ and _____ make _____

_____ and _____ make _____

8. Try combining three different colors. Unless you have three hands, this will be easier if a friend helps.

Explanation

If you've ever messed around mixing colors with crayons or paints, you probably have an idea what happens when you mix colors. You know: red and blue make purple, yellow and blue make green, etc. Most of the time with the spotlights, though, you didn't get the usual results. That's because combining different colored lights on a white surface is not the same as mixing paint or crayon pigments on that same white surface.

To understand what's going on, you need to know that light moves like a wave. It's sort of like an ocean wave. Waves come in different wavelengths and are measured from the top of one wave to the top of the next one. Short wavelengths are scrunched together and long wavelengths are spread out. Light comes in lots of wavelengths and our eyes can detect some of them. No big surprise that those wavelengths are called the visible wavelengths. Short, visible wavelengths of light are violet to us and long, visible wavelengths of light appear red. All the other colors of the rainbow are in between. They compose the **visible spectrum**.

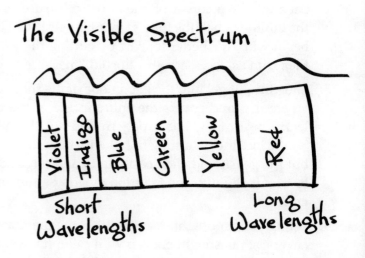

If you combine all the wavelengths of light in the visible spectrum, you get **white light**. Gels (also called light filters) don't combine wavelengths, they remove some of the wavelengths from white light to create colored light.

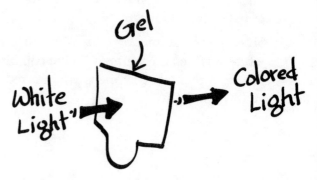

Gels act like windows that allow only certain wavelengths, or colors, of light to pass. In science lingo, this is called the **transmittance** of light through the gels. It's usually given as a percentage of transmittance with 100%T as letting all of that color through the object. You can draw a graph that shows just what colors a gel will let through. For example, a really good blue gel would let all of the blue light through and no other colors. Its graph might look like the one on the left. It lets zero light through at all other wavelengths and 100 percent of the light through at the blue wavelengths. The blue gel in your kit isn't quite this good. Its graph looks like the one on the right, but it also lets some violet, green, yellow, orange and red light through.

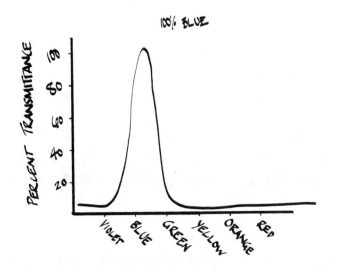
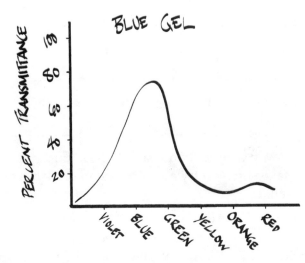

The yellow gel transmits light from blue to red, but the mixture still appears yellow. If you combine or add the yellow gel's graph with the blue gel's graph, which is what happens when you shine the two lights on a white surface, it results in a graph that contains almost all colors. That's why adding light from the yellow and blue filters produces not green, but white light. Adding more colors produces a better and better white, because adding more colors fills in the gaps of the missing wavelengths.

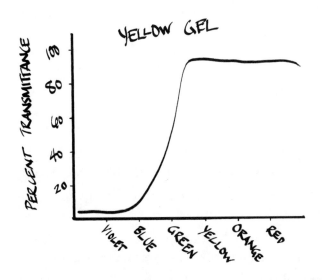
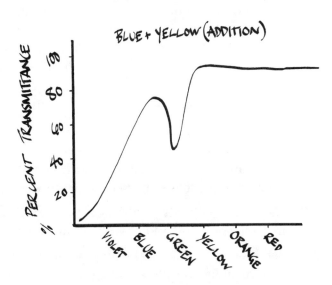

Science Fair Survival Techniques

Procedure

Instead of combining the effects of gels, now you're going to subtract their effects. You'll need only one spotlight for this. Either that, or just look through the gels at a light source. **Never look directly at the sun!**

1. Head back to the dark room and shine your spotlight onto a white surface.

2. Put different combinations of gels in your spotlight, so the light goes through both gels. Record the colors you get.

    _____ plus _____ gives _____ light

    _____ plus _____ gives _____ light

    _____ plus _____ gives _____ light

    _____ plus _____ gives _____ light

    _____ plus _____ gives _____ light

    _____ plus _____ gives _____ light

3. Now, try more than just two gels. Some of the three- and four-gel combinations are kinda pretty. Make sure you try all six gels at once. Uh, you may have to perform some repairs on the tube. Oh, well...

More Explanation

In Procedure 1 when you mixed colored lights from different flashlights, you were adding the colors together. Each flashlight gives more light. As you put more gels in front of each other on the same flashlight, they take away more light. This subtraction process leads to the kind of color combinations you probably expected in Scene 1.

Look at what happens when you put a blue gel in front of a yellow gel. The yellow gel lets light pass according to its graph. The blue gel lets light pass according to its graph.

Light will get through only if it can pass through both gels (remember, they act like windows). The only light that can get through both gels is shown below. Compare this with the graph for the green gel at the end of this booklet. This stuff is amazing!

Subtracting other colors works the same way. It should make sense to you why using all the gels cuts out most of the light and you get a dark brown or black "light."

Now you have two ways to get light on stage. The first way is by adding different colors from multiple lights. The second way is by putting different gels in front of each other using one light source to create new colors. You can then add these new colors together to get even more variations. The science fun never stops!

Extension Ideas

1. Try shining different-colored spotlights on your face as you look in a mirror in a dark room. Notice how different colors create different moods. How can you affect the audience with colored lighting?

2. Use your spotlights to **add** colors you couldn't add before. Try making magenta (red and violet gels in same spotlight) and green (yellow and blue gels in the same spotlight).

3. Set three spotlights on the floor or table so they shine at the same white spot on the wall. Make sure they're aimed at different angles. Put a yellow gel in one, a red gel in another, and a blue gel in the third. Wave your hand in front of the wall so the spotlights cast shadows on the wall. Figure out why each shadow is the color it is.

Earthbake

The earth is made up of various layers of material that start at the core and extend out into space. To build our earth, let's start at the center and work outward. So roll up your sleeves, put on your apron, and let's do some terra-forming.

The **inner core** is the center most region of the earth. Most scientists believe it's composed of solid nickel and iron, while the outer core is a liquid iron layer. The core generates the magnetic field of the earth and has an estimated temperature of about 5000°F (degrees Fahrenheit). Surrounding the outer core is the semi-molten mantle which makes up the largest part of the earth. The very outside layer of the earth is called the crust and it's only a few miles thick. It is very similar to a pie crust in that it's thin, hard, dry, and crumbles. The crust is the part of the earth we live on and anytime the crust moves, the result is an earthquake. All in all, the earth is a little less than 8,000 miles across.

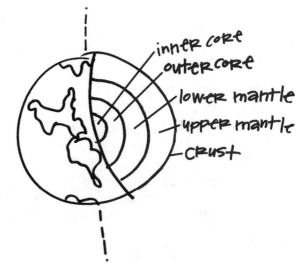

Materials

2 rubber hemispheres (poppers)	1 protractor
1 bottle of iron filings	1 rod magnet
1 metal nut	1 stick of blue clay
1 length of string	1 stick of green clay

Procedure

1. Grab the piece of string. You are going to use the string to represent the axis of the earth. That is, a line that passes from the north to the south geographic poles. Fortunately, it's imaginary and doesn't create any concern or property damage for Santa Claus.

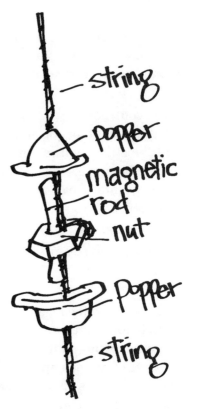

2. Grab the metal nut and thread the nut on the string. You may want to find the middle of the string and tie the nut to it. This nut can be thought of as the inner core of the earth. The inner core is extremely dense and very hot. It is thought to be a solid sphere about 1600 miles across under a pressure close to 50 million pounds per square inch. That's compared with the 14.70 pounds per square inch at sea level that we're used to from the atmosphere.

The core generates the magnetic field of the earth, so take the nut and string combination and slip the rod magnet into the nut, next to the string. Then, center the nut on the magnet. Use the illustration to the right as a guide. When you've done this step, the inner core is complete.

© 1997 Rev 1999 The Wild Goose Co. **Science Fair Survival Techniques**

3. Most geologists believe the outer core is made up of a liquid iron layer that is about 1300 miles thick. You'll use iron filings to represent this layer. Take out one of the rubber popper hemispheres and thread it onto the bottom end of the string, cup-side up. You may want to use the end of the rod magnet to help push the string through the hole in the popper. Once you have threaded the popper, slide it onto the end of the rod magnet so that it cups the nut at the middle of the magnet. You might have to work a little to get the popper over the rod magnet. You should now have a string and a rod going through the little hole in the rubber popper. Now, take the second popper and thread it onto the other end of the string in the same way, but leave it at the end of the magnet until the next step. Check out the drawings on the previous page.

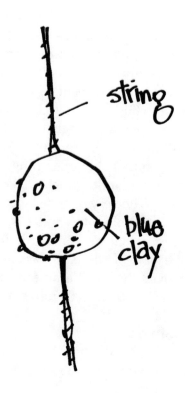

4. Open up your bottle of iron filings, carefully fill the rubber popper at the center of the magnet with the filings, and recap the bottle. Then slide the top popper toward the middle of the magnet until it encloses the nut and iron filings or the <u>core</u> of your earth.

5. Once the "core" is contained in the poppers, clean off any extra iron filings on the magnet. What you just made with the rubber poppers is the lower mantle of the earth enclosing the inner and outer core. The lower mantle is a 1200 mile thick layer and is thought to be made of the same stuff throughout. Scientists like to call this a homogeneous composition.

6. Push your newly made lower mantle/core combo into the center of the blue clay with the string hanging out of the top and bottom. Again, the magnet will represent the magnetic poles of the earth and the string will represent the geographic poles of the earth. Remember: the north pole of the magnet you marked should be on the southern half of your model close to the string. Now, shape the clay into a ball around the core and lower mantle. Be sure the string dangles from both geographic poles and that the diameter of the clay ball matches the length of the magnet.

   The clay will represent the upper mantle of the earth, about a 600 mile thickness in the official planet. The mantle makes up the greatest volume of the earth and is composed mostly of molten silicate rocks.

7. The string and the magnet represent the geographic and magnetic poles. The poles "stick out" of the earth in four different places, so if you took an X-ray of your earth ball, you would see the string and magnet crossing in the middle of the inner core. On your model, the "two" north poles should be about ³⁄₁₆ of an inch apart on the surface. The same is true of the "two" south poles. Ideally, your magnetic pole is 12 degrees away from the corresponding geographic pole — but that's hard to do with string and clay.

You can approximate the poles' positions by using your protractor (that semicircular piece of plastic with numbers on the edge). Figure out where 78 degrees would be located on the protractor (that's 12 degrees from vertical). Position the protractor so that the 0-180 line is halfway between the north and south magnetic poles with its cross hair viewed as being in the center of the earth and the 90 degree angle in line with the magnet. If you want, you can keep the protractor in place by pushing it into the clay. Now, gently smoosh and moosh (very highly technical terms) the string through the clay so that the string is oriented at the 78 degree mark. This should result in the axis having a 12 degree tilt from the magnetic pole. Flip the world upside down and do the same thing with the southern poles, but remember to keep the axis in a straight line through the earth. Press the clay firmly around the string and magnet to hold everything in place, then make the earth ball nice and round again. The figure on page 12 should help with this one.

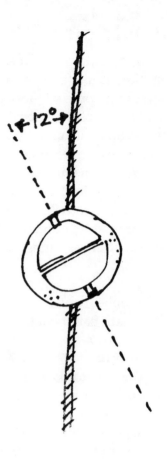

8. OK, time to put the crust on the earth. The blue clay will double as the oceans of the earth. After all, it is the color seen from space. With the green clay, You'll make the continents of the earth. So follow a picture of the earth and construct some landforms to match. Silicates make up about 90 percent of the earth's crust, so it is very appropriate to make the crust out of the common silicate known as clay. However, there is something you should know about the crust: it's the thinnest layer on the earth. It's thinner than an egg shell is to an egg. It's about like the skin of an apple in comparison to the apple. It's only about four miles thick under the ocean and about 25 miles thick under the continents — not a whole bunch of crust when you think about it. So you don't need to make the green land very thick.

9. If you hold the earth by its axis (the string), then you can test drive your earth by giving it a gentle spin from left to right (west to east). The real earth is actually spinning quite fast. It rotates at 18.5 miles per second or about 1,000 miles per hour. You won't notice it because you're so small compared to the earth. Since your model is so small; however, it will appear not to be moving at all in real time. Remember: it takes one whole day (24 hours) for earth to make one complete rotation. Because of this spin, the earth bulges slightly at the equator. If you squeeze the earth at the poles, flattening the earth ball slightly, you can simulate this bulge.

Pinstriping the Globe

In order to pinpoint exact locations on the earth's surface, people developed **latitude** (north/south) and **longitude** (east/west) lines. These are imaginary lines on the earth that cross at regular intervals and can be precisely located. The **equator** divides the northern from the southern hemisphere and is marked as "zero degrees latitude." As you travel north or south, latitude is measured from zero degrees at the equator to ninety degrees at the geographic poles. Longitude, on the other hand, is measured from zero degrees to 180 degrees (a half-circle) either to the east or the west and divides the eastern from the western hemispheres. "Zero degrees longitude" is called the **Prime Meridian** and runs from the geographic North Pole through Greenwich, England, (the site of the old Royal Observatory where I used to hang out) into West Africa, and down to the geographic South Pole. Exactly opposite (at 180 degrees east or west longitude) in the Pacific Ocean is the **International Dateline.** This is where all days have their official beginning. That's why it can be Monday in the United States and Tuesday in Japan.

Materials
5 rubber bands
1 earth ball model

top view

earth w/ longitude bands

Procedure
1. The equator is an imaginary line on the surface of the earth that marks the halfway point between the north and south geographic poles. It also represents zero degrees latitude. The equator is perpendicular to the axis of the earth. While holding the north end of the string axis of your earth ball, figure out where the equator should be located and stretch a rubber band evenly around your model as its equator. Try not to squash too many homes!

2. After you've put on the equator, you can place the longitude lines. The longitude lines are perpendicular to the equator that you just put on the earth ball. Longitude runs from the geographic north pole to the geographic south pole. Using a second rubber band, evenly stretch it around your earth from the geographic north pole to the geographic south pole. It should touch the string twice, once at each pole.

3. Slip on another longitude rubber band, but this time position it ninety degrees to the first one. It should also be ninety degrees to the equator. Remember, it must pass through both geographic poles.

4. If you look at your earth model straight down on one of the poles, you'll see a cross, like someone is cutting a pie into fourths. Put on the next two longitude lines (rubber bands) so that they cut this pie into even wedges. You should end up with an earth that looks like it is a peeled orange with eight identical sections. Use the illustration on the previous page as a guide.

5. Take another look at the latitude and longitude lines you just put on your earth. Identify the equator, prime meridian, International Date Line, 45 degrees east and west longitude, 90 degrees east and west longitude, and 135 degrees east and west longitude. No way you can get lost now.

Gooey Glue Globs

Materials

   1 bottle of sodium tetraborate, 2%
   1 bottle of food coloring (optional)
   1 bottle of glue solution (50% school glue & 50% water)
   1 bowl
   1 craft stick
   1 pipette
   1 plastic bag
   paper towels

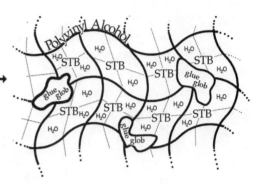

$$CH_2 - CH - CH_2 - CH - CH_2 - CH \text{ (aq)} + Na_2B_4O_7 \text{ (aq)} \rightarrow$$

   OH   OH   OH   *Sodium Tetraborate*
       Polyvinyl Alcohol   *(STB)*

Procedure

1. Shake the glue solution <u>vigorously</u>! This stuff settles like crazy. Pour half the bottle of glue solution into your bowl. Put the cap back on the bottle. Accident prevention, you know.

2. If you'd like to tint your polymer, add 4-5 drops of food coloring to the glue solution and give it a good stir.

3. Using the pipette, add one milliliter of sodium tetraborate to the glue solution by filling the pipette to the top of the four lines. Add two or three more milliliters of sodium tetraborate. Stir vigorously with the craft stick until a glob starts to form. The glob collects on the stick after 15-20 seconds of stirring. Lift it out of the bowl. If there's a lot of liquid left in your cup, add another milliliter of sodium tetraborate, put the glob back, and stir again.

4. Remove the semisolid glob from the craft stick with your fingers, place it in your hands, and roll it around to dry it off a little bit. It will remain sticky for 1-2 minutes and eventually it takes on an elastic quality. Bounce it, stretch it, play with it, and see what it'll do.

5. When you're done with your glob, store it in a bag and put it in the refrigerator to last longer. This is a water-rich polymer and there are lots of bacteria that have just jumped off of your hands onto your new colloid. It's a great place for them to grow if it's warm enough.

6. Wash out your bowl, your pipette and craft stick so you can use them again. Use the paper towels to clean up.

On Your Own

Explanation

Please, let me explain. A **polymer** may be described as a repeating sequence of molecular units. Start with a single molecule, it's a **monomer.** Join two of them, you'll have a **dimer**, three a **trimer**, . . . Connect a whole bunch of them together, it's a **polymer.** Most of what you'll be holding in your hand is water because water is the bridge between the molecules. In this case, there are globs of white glue proteins stuck in there, too. The sodium tetraborate you add "clumps" the polyvinyl alcohol polymers with the white glue globs on the front and back, top and bottom, and left and right, forming a three-dimensional polymer that might be classified as a semisolid gel. All this is done very quickly and the result of the process is a rubbery colloid.

Glue was invented way back when things needed to be stuck together. It's made from insoluble proteins (collagens) found in the connective tissues of mammals, which is why horses don't like jokes about glue factories. Glue also contains polyvinyl alcohol which is the connecting polymer in this reaction.

Sodium tetraborate, or borax as it's better known, finds itself on the shelves of many grocery stores as a laundry detergent additive. It's also used to cure hides, fireproof fabrics, and to control cockroaches.

Slime à la Mode

Materials

      polyvinyl alcohol, 2%
      sodium tetraborate, 2%
1 bowl
1 craft stick
1 pipette

Procedure

1. Shake the polyvinyl alcohol and pour two tablespoons into your bowl. Take a look at it and give it a stir or two. Notice any changes that occurred? Rub a small amount between your thumb and index finger. It'll start out cool and wet, but soon it becomes sticky and dirty lumps start showing up. That's called the booger stage and means the polyvinyl has pulled off dirt and dead skin from your fingers. Keep rubbing and soon the "boogers" will fall off and your skin will feel smooth and soft.

2. Measure out one milliliter of sodium tetraborate solution and squirt it into the bowl containing the polyvinyl alcohol. Stir quickly with the craft stick to produce the slime. If your slime is a little runny, add another half milliliter or so and then stir again. If you add too much, your slime will get thick and "crumbly."

3. Examine the properties of the cross-linked polymer (play with the stuff). Let it flow from your fingers. Hold it up to your nose and smile at anyone close by. It's especially effective if you fake a sneeze. Add a glop of shaving cream on top, and you'll have Slime à la Mode!

4. When you're all done, you can save the slime by putting it in a plastic bag. Toss it in the fridge for longer life or let it dry in the bowl and observe that reaction. It takes several days to dry out.

Explanation

    The basic reaction is the same as the one in *Gooey Glue Globs*, only there are no glue globs (collagens) floating around to be included. Imagine the polyvinyl alcohol molecules to be tiny steel chains in a bowl. Each link of the chain is a vinyl alcohol unit or monomer. When all the links are hooked together, you have the polymer polyvinyl alcohol. If you want to, you can pull each chain out one at a time. But if you throw a few small, powerful magnets into the bowl, and then try to pull one chain out of the bowl, you'll drag the rest of them with it. That's sort of what the sodium tetraborate does to the polyvinyl alcohol polymers. It pulls them out of the bowl all at once so that you end up with a slow-moving, glistening mass that feels cool to the touch. That's because it's endothermic, drawing heat from its surroundings including your hand.

Polyvinyl alcohol is used by the plastic industry to form surface coatings and to make films resistant to gasoline. It is also used to make artificial sponges, hoses, and printing inks. If you look inside your contact lens wetting solutions, you'll find this stuff lubricating the lenses.

Sodium tetraborate is used in the wood industry to protect against fungus and to make new wood look old. It's used to solder metals as well as to glaze and enamel pottery. It also has medicinal uses.

$$CH_2 - CH - CH_2 - CH - CH_2 - CH \ (aq) \ + \ Na_2B_4O_7 \ (aq) \ \rightarrow$$

OH   OH   OH   *Sodium Tetraborate*

Polyvinyl Alcohol   *(STB)*

Carbo Goo

Materials
    2 hands (yours will work fine)
      cornstarch
      water

$$O - C_6H_{10}O_5 - O - C_6H_{10}O_5 - (solid) + H_2O \rightarrow \text{Colloidal Starch (aq)}$$

      Starch Molecule

Procedure
1. Pour a small pile (about 2 tablespoons) of cornstarch into one hand.

2. Dip the fingers of your other hand into some water and "dribble" a tiny amount onto the cornstarch. As you dribble, work the water into the cornstarch and add a little at a time until you have made a ball. Keep your fingers moving and pressing.

3. When you can press a ball of cornstarch in your fingers, you've added enough water. Squeeze hard and pick up the ball in your fingers. Hold it over your open hand and stop squeezing. You'll notice that the "solid" ball of cornstarch becomes a colloid and dribbles down into your other hand. Play with it all you want.

4. With the pile of starch in one palm, try pressing as hard as you can with your other thumb into the center of the pile. This will force the water out from the starch and leave a fairly dry clump in your palm.

5. What happens if you add a lot more water to the cornstarch?

6. When you're done, put the cornstarch in the garbage and clean up with water. It's best to do this activity over a sink because it usually makes a big mess. If it does happen to spill, help clean it up! Don't forget to wash your paws!

Explanation
When the starch is mixed with a small amount of water, it forms a goo that runs all over your hand. That's right, a colloid or, in this case, a sol, which is a solid dispersed in a liquid. When you lightly squeeze on the goo, it forces the long starch molecules closer together. This traps the water in-between the starch chains and forms a semirigid structure. When the pressure is released, the starch begins to flow again. If it is held in the palm of the hand, and as more pressure is applied, the water can be forced from the starch molecules leaving a stiff clump. But, if additional water is added, a complete dispersion occurs.

Starch is used in foods to help thicken liquids. It's what makes a gravy "stick to your ribs." In the pharmaceutical industry, starch is used as a filler and binder in tablets. It makes a great paste, keeps your clothes from falling over in wrinkled heaps, and is an antidote for iodine poisoning.